ספר קיבוץ גלויות

Sefer Kibbutz Galuyos

The Mitzvah to Return
to Eretz Yisrael
Before Moshiach Comes

by Rabbi Chananya Weissman

Copyright © 2025 Rabbi Chananya Weissman

All rights reserved. Permission granted to reproduce and distribute free of charge for personal and educational use. Selling without prior written consent prohibited. In all cases this notice must remain intact.

ISBN: 978-1-7354138-0-8

www.chananyaweissman.com

CONTENTS

Introduction..1
What it means to go up like a wall.....................................4
The meaning of Hashem taking an oath............................9
The Early Zionists and the Three Oaths..........................11
Hashem may use wicked people to perform His miracles.........13
Chazal's presumption that Torah scholars wouldn't stay behind..................................18
The excuses ring hollow and contradict Chazal.............20
Wicked leadership is not an excuse to abandon the land.........23
One needs a heter to LEAVE Eretz Yisrael......................25
It is excruciating to leave Eretz Yisrael even if one must do so........................26
Settling Eretz Yisrael takes precedence............................27
A *mitzvah* even during the period of exile....................30
Treasuring cattle more than souls....................................32
Moshiach comes after the ingathering............................35
Hashem's promise is fulfilled even if we return on our own....41
Returning to good includes returning to Eretz Yisrael..............44
Incomplete joy precedes Moshiach..................................48
The stragglers wait for Moshiach.....................................50
Mitzvos without reward in *galus*..................................51
Eretz Yisrael is not a cemetery, but our homeland........53
A *mitzvah* even in our times..57
A wise move...65
How can strictly religious Jews forsake living in Eretz Yisrael?.........................67
A *mitzvah* to help others move to Eretz Yisrael............69
Worth more than all the money in the world................73

Like a portion in the world to come..76

It's difficult to permit leaving Eretz Yisrael even for a *mitzvah*..77

The insanity of leaving Eretz Yisrael...79

Contradicting our own prayers..81

It's not supposed to be easy..84

The *yetzer hara* to remain in *galus*..85

The excuse of seeking a safer land..87

Three generations in Eretz Yisrael before Moshiach...................89

It's all part of Hashem's plan..92

"Distinguished children"..95

Afterword...97

Appendix..99

Go Up Like a Wall, Chapter 14 Returning Like a Wall............100

Why God Chose the Early Zionists...107

What Mordechai Teaches the *Galus* Jew......................................114

What's Your *Galus* Exit Plan?..117

The Foolish Prisoner...127

The *Galus* Money Trap..129

The Anti-Semitism Handbook for Diaspora Jews.......................133

The Secret Behind the *Galus* Jew..138

Courting Israel...144

Relating to Israel Under the Erev Rav..147

Introduction

The notion of Jews leaving *galus*, let alone en masse, was not a practical consideration for most of the last two thousand years. It required deep faith that Hashem could bring redemption in the blink of an eye and perform miracles that stretched the limits of one's imagination. This was true even during fleeting periods of respite from persecution; picking up and moving to Eretz Yisrael was simply not a realistic option for the average Jew.

In the last century that has completely changed. Practically every Jew in the world can realistically live in Eretz Yisrael if he so chooses. The sacrifices and complications that he might face are significant and should not be downplayed, but they pale in comparison to those his ancestors faced.

The realistic possibility of Jews leaving *galus*, whether individually or en masse, raises serious theological questions. These questions that were once theoretical have become practical, and every Jew who strives to live in accordance with the Torah must face them. If we are not to dismiss the rejuvenation of Jewish life in Israel as a theologically insignificant event — and how can we? — then those who choose to remain in *galus* — and it IS a choice — must find support from the Torah for their decision.

After all, the Jew who remains in *galus* continuously davens for Hashem to gather in the exiles, yet consciously forgoes the opportunity to join the millions of Jews who represent the fulfillment of these prayers. One way or another, he needs to justify his decision.

The clever Jewish mind, well aware of the seeming incongruence between his prayers, the unfolding of Jewish history, and his decision to stubbornly remain in *galus* indefinitely, has come up with endless justifications. The *galus* Jew can rattle off so many reasons to live anywhere in the world, no matter what, except in Eretz Yisrael, that it gives the impression that Eretz Yisrael is somehow the worst place on earth a Jew could ever be, God forbid.

Many "religious" Jews actually believe this, for a variety of creative reasons, and they claim the Torah squarely supports them.

The more "moderate" *galus* Jew believes that living in Eretz Yisrael is just another lifestyle choice, nothing more. Needless to say, it doesn't fit his lifestyle.

The more spiritually inclined *galus* Jew will acknowledge that it's "a dream" to live in Eretz Yisrael "someday," but will insist that it is a practical impossibility for a long list of reasons that he makes little to no effort to overcome. As far as he is concerned, there is certainly no theological imperative to move to Eretz Yisrael, or at least to seriously attempt to overcome the obstacles on his list, and it is therefore Hashem's decision that he will remain in *galus* until Moshiach comes or the end of time (whichever comes first), and not his own.

Although the vast majority of Torah scholarship is once again in Eretz Yisrael, where it is meant to be, *galus* Jews too have rabbis who support their worldview. It is therefore easy for them to dismiss any and all Torah-based arguments against their choice. When push comes to shove, the Jew who has already made up his mind and found a rabbi to lean upon — even if the Jew doesn't know what this rabbi says about anything else and doesn't care — will play the "Da'as Torah" card, and that's the end of it. The "Da'as Torah" card is an impenetrable shield, an automatic victory, or at least a respectable stalemate, in any Torah discussion.

This sort of Jew should stop reading here, for virtually no one can convince him to change his mind. Any attempt at intelligent, productive discussion will quickly turn wearisome and will inevitably stall at the same dead end: "I'm following Da'as Torah." So what is the point of studying and discussing Torah sources?

The sort of Jew, however, who engages in critical thinking, and in fact believes critical thinking is a religious imperative combined with submission to rabbinic authority to a certain extent, must familiarize himself with the pertinent Torah sources, of which there are many. Decisions on Jewish law, practice, and thought are not to be made based on sound bites, a single cherry-picked source taken out of context, or mindless appeals to authority. Rabbinic authority is not a substitute for our being informed, educated, independently thoughtful people; it is to guide us in cases of doubt.

I believe a study of the pertinent Torah sources leaves no room for doubt.

Barring exceptional circumstances, living in Eretz Yisrael today is not only permitted, but is strongly preferred, a tremendous merit and *mitzvah*, to the point of being a religious imperative — before Moshiach comes.

Let's clear our mind of the sound bites and see what the Torah and Chazal actually have to say.

What it means to go up like a wall

The ideology that downplays, discourages, or even prohibits Jews from returning to Eretz Yisrael en masse before Moshiach comes hinges almost entirely on a single source from Chazal: The three oaths. Before examining this source, the following principles should be kept in mind:

1) When a mountain of Torah sources all point in one direction, and a single Torah source seems to point in the other direction, it is senseless and intellectually dishonest to disregard the mountain of Torah sources and build an entire ideology based on the outlier.

It is also highly unlikely that the exception represents a disagreement among Chazal unless explicitly stated — especially when dealing with something fundamental, about which there should be no doubt. Hence, neither of the seemingly conflicting sources should be dismissed or explained away; every attempt should be made to reconcile them.

The honest, sensible student of Torah will acknowledge that the mountain of Torah sources represents the primary position that should guide our thoughts and practice most of the time, while the exception is there to add context and balance the position. The exception must be reconciled with the majority so it fits in its proper place, thereby achieving harmony between all the sources and arriving at a clear understanding of the Torah's instruction.

2) It is remarkable that none of the codifiers of *halacha* in the generations following the Talmudic period — most notably the Rif, the Rosh, and the Rambam — transmitted to us a *halacha* that we are forbidden to return to Eretz Yisrael before Moshiach comes, nor any indication to that effect based on the Midrashic source about the oaths. There is no area of Jewish law and life

that was too insignificant for them to cover — yet a presumed prohibition to return to Eretz Yisrael either individually or en masse completely escaped them? Are we supposed to believe it was too obvious for them to bother mentioning? Especially considering the supposedly great importance of remaining in *galus* until Moshiach comes? It's incredible.

There is no comparable omission from our primary codifiers of *halacha* that would lend credence to such an argument.

Indeed, not only should they have codified such a *halacha*, they should have outlined for us the details and boundaries. After all, there was a Jewish presence in Eretz Yisrael throughout the last two thousand years. How many Jews are allowed to live there without violating an oath? Under what circumstances may one voluntarily move to Eretz Yisrael? We should expect at least a chapter in the Rambam's Mishneh Torah, and detailed *halachic* responsa throughout the ages, rounding out the details of the oath to remain in *galus*...yet there is no such literature.

Much has already been written about the three oaths mentioned in Kesubos 111a and Shir HaShirim Rabba 2:7. I devoted a chapter of *Go Up Like a Wall* to a detailed treatment of these sources, and have included that in the appendix.

The most essential point is that the oath not to go up like a wall (or in a wall, according to another version) is explained by the commentators almost with one voice to refer to leaving the *galus* en masse, with force, in an act of rebellion.

For example, Rashi writes:

ביד חזקה כולם יחד.

With a strong hand [force], all together.

The term יעלו חומה comes from Yoel 2:7, where it refers to scaling a wall or otherwise conquering a walled area with force. It is not for nothing that Chazal specifically chose this term to describe the oath.

As Rav David Luria writes:

הלשון יעלו חומה האמור כאן (ולהלן ב:ז) יצא מלשון המקרא (יואל ב) "כאנשי מלחמה יעלו חומה", והכוונה שלא יעלו כלם ביד חזקה (והראשונה שלא ימרדו כל המלכיות היינו שבארץ גלותם עצמם יהיו נאמנים למלכות ולא ישתתפו ח"ו עם מורדים במלכות.).

The term "go up like a wall" stated here comes from the language of the verse (Yoel 2:7) "Like men of war they will go up like a wall." The meaning is that they should not all go up with force. (And the first oath, that they should not rebel against the kingdoms, means that in the actual lands of their exile they should be loyal to the kingdom and not join, God forbid, with those who rebel against the kingdom.)

The Yefe Kol also explains:

פירוש, לא לבד שלא ימרדו בחוקות המלכות להמלט ממסים וארנוניות, אבל גם להתקבץ ולנוס מהארץ אשר המה יושבים בקרבה, השביע להם הקב"ה שלא יעשו כזאת.

The meaning is that not only should they not rebel against the laws of the kingdom to escape from being forced to pay personal and property taxes, but also to gather and flee from the land in which they reside — Hashem adjured them not to do such a thing.

It is not our place to decide that the period of exile shall end now and attempt to force the issue unilaterally, without a clear sign from Hashem. In fact, even attempting to force the issue through "too much" prayer is prohibited by another of the oaths (as Rashi in Kesubos explains the primary version of this oath). We must achieve redemption through *teshuva* (or, if necessary, expiation of our sins through suffering, God forbid) and spiritual merits, combined with Hashem's mercy. Attempting to force the issue either physically or spiritually is an act of rebellion against Hashem's will — even if done with the best of intentions.

As Chazal teach at the end of Shir Hashirim Rabba, 8:12:

נמשלה גאולתן של ישראל בקציר ובבציר בבשמים ובילדה. בקציר, הדא חקלא כד היא מחצדא בלא ענתה אפילו תבנא לית הוא טב, בענתה הוא טב, הדא הוא דכתיב (יואל ד:יג) "שלחו מגל כי בשל קציר." נמשלה בבציר הדין כרמא כד מקטיף בלא ענתיה אפילו בסמיה לית הוא טב,

בענתיה הוא טב, כך (ישעיה כז:ב) "כרם חמר ענו לה" איתעביד כרמא חמר זמר לה. נמשלה בבשמים, מה בשמים הללו כשהן נלקטין כשהן רכין לחים אין ריחם נודף, כשהן יבשים ונלקטין ריחן נודף. נמשלה כיולדה, הדא איתתא כד ילדה כלא ענתה לא חייא ולדא. כד ילדת בענתה חיי, כך כתיב (מיכה ה:ב) "לכן יתנם עד עת יולדה ילדה" ר' אחא בשם ר' יהושע בן לוי אמר (ישעיה ס:כב) "אני ה' בעתה אחישנה", לא זכיתם – בעתה. זכיתם – אחישנה. כן יהי רצון במהרה בימינו אמן.

The redemption of Israel is metaphorically equated with a grain harvest, a grape harvest, spices, and a woman giving birth. With a grain harvest, for when a field is harvested before its time, even the straw is not good, but in its time it is good, as it is written, (Yoel 4:13) "Send forth the sickle, for the harvest has ripened."

It is likened to a grape harvest, for when a vineyard is harvested before its time, even the vinegar from it is not good, but in its time it is good. So [it is written], (Yeshaya 27:2) "A vineyard of fine wine, they will praise it." When the vineyard is ready to produce wine, pluck it.

It is likened to spices, for just as when spices are gathered when they are soft and moist, their scent does not waft, but if they are gathered when dry, their scent wafts.

It is likened to a woman giving birth, for when a woman gives birth before the proper time, the child doesn't live. When she gives birth in the proper time they live. So it is written, (Micha 5:2) "Therefore He will leave them until the time of the mother to give birth." Rabbi Acha said in the name of Rabbi Yehoshua, (Yeshaya 60:22) "I am Hashem, in its time I will hasten it." If you do not merit, [it will come] in its time. If you merit, I will hasten it. So it should be His will, quickly in our days, Amen.

Attempting to force the redemption in an improper way, before its proper time, will only have deleterious results, God forbid.

The Etz Yosef adds a critical qualifier to the oath not to go up like a wall, which, as we will see, is consistently expressed by Chazal in numerous places.

He writes:

לשון זה הוא מפסוק (יואל ב:ז) "כאנשי מלחמה יעלו חומה", והכוונה שלא יעלו כולם ביד חזקה, ורצה לומר ודאי דרשות לכל אחד מישראל

לעלות לארץ ישראל, אלא שלא יעלו יחד ביד חזקה (רש"א) שחלילה לנו זאת עד יערה רוח חסד ממרום וישלח ישועה על ידי משיחו ובהרשאה מן מלך יושב מרום, ועיין לקמן פ"ח סימן י"א ועיין פרק קמא דיומא.

This term is from the verse in Yoel (2:7)"Like men of war they will go up like a wall," and the meaning is that they should not go up all together with a strong hand. This means to say that every individual from Israel certainly has the right to go up to Eretz Yisrael, but they should not go up together with force. Far be it from us to do this until a spirit of kindness descends from above and He will send His salvation through His anointed one, and with the permission of the King who dwells above....

Clearly there is no prohibition for individuals to return to Eretz Yisrael before Moshiach comes; this in no way violates an oath or Hashem's will. There is also no limit stated or implied regarding how many Jews go up before Moshiach comes; it is unreasonable to argue that we cannot go together and get a group rate. The only issue is to raise an army in exile and force the issue before Hashem sends Moshiach to take the (remaining) Jews out of exile, after which force will be permitted if necessary.

None of the millions of Jews living in Eretz Yisrael raised an army to fight their way out of *galus* or fight their way into Eretz Yisrael, nor would the overwhelming majority of Jews in *galus* need to do so now. Living in Eretz Yisrael today is not an act of rebellion against Hashem's will, nor is moving there — even if done in large numbers, in an organized fashion.

By all means, go with others and get a group rate.

The meaning of Hashem taking an oath

The language of Hashem taking an oath, or imposing an oath on others, indicates a decree from Hashem for how He will run the world, not the imposition of a *mitzvah* per se. This is clearly evident throughout Tanach when the term is used. For example, Yeshaya 14:24 states:

נשבע ה' צבאות לאמר אם לא כאשר דמיתי כן היתה וכאשר יעצתי היא תקום.

Hashem the Lord of Hosts took an oath saying, As I intended, so it was, and just as I have planned, so it will be fulfilled.

Ibn Ezra explains:

שבועת השם היא הגזרה שנגזרה.

The oath of Hashem is the decree that has been decreed.

Accordingly, Hashem made a decree that we shall not and cannot force the end of the exile by leaving *galus* with force. This certainly indicates that we should not attempt to do so, and that such attempts will incur harsh consequences. It is not a *halacha* in the typical sense — individual Jews are not banned from returning to Eretz Yisrael if they have the opportunity — but guidance for the Jewish people as a whole in how to approach the punishment that was decreed upon them.

Returning to Eretz Yisrael in a way that does not go against Hashem's will is not only permissible, but a fulfillment of Hashem's decree. When we have the opportunity to return en masse in a way that does not violate Hashem's will, it is a clear sign from Hashem that we should not miss.

The Early Zionists and the Three Oaths

Some argue that the early Zionists violated the oaths by declaring a state. This is highly questionable on many grounds:

- They were granted the right to a state by the ruling powers of the world, including those who occupied and controlled Eretz Yisrael at the time.
- The wars they fought were defensive in nature, not specifically intended to conquer Eretz Yisrael. Jews have the right to defend themselves from attack wherever they may be, including in *galus*, and have every right to do so in an organized fashion.
- It is appropriate and preferable for Jews to govern themselves to the greatest extent possible, whether in Eretz Yisrael or in *galus*. There is no prohibition for masses of Jews who live in Eretz Yisrael to govern themselves. The notion that they must seek out *goyim* to rule over them and the land is preposterous and obscene.

However, even if one argues that the early Zionists did violate an oath — and there are reasonable grounds for such a position — so what? It would be the least of the sins these generally wicked gangsters committed. What does that have to do with us? Whatever they did, they did. It does not pasul the land indefinitely until Moshiach comes, sends us out, tears down everything they did, cleanses the land, and only then allows us to return. That notion, too, is preposterous and obscene.

Lehavdil, the lands of Ammon and Moav that the Jews in the times of Moshe were prohibited from conquering were "purified" when Sichon conquered them first, and we subsequently conquered the land from them. And although we were prohibited from rebuilding the city of Yericho, once Hiel rebuilt it and paid the price, anyone was allowed to settle there. So if the early Zionists violated an oath or two, that is their problem, and it has no bearing on our right/*mitzvah* to return to Eretz Yisrael.

The theological question of why Hashem would bring the Jewish people back to Eretz Yisrael largely through the actions of thoroughly wicked people is addressed in an article I wrote called Why God Chose the Early Zionists, based on two answers offered in Eim Habanim Semeicha and two additional answers. The article is copied in the appendix as well.

Either way, whether we like the answers or not, whether we understand Hashem's ways at least in part or not, our right/*mitzvah* to return to Eretz Yisrael is not affected by what the early Zionists did long ago.

Hashem may use wicked people to perform His miracles

As the Midrash on Shir Hashirim 5:3 states:

"דודי שלח ידו מן החור...." אמר ר' אבא בר כהנא וכי מה טיבו של חור זה להיות מגדל שרצים? אלא כך אמרה כנסת ישראל לפני הקדוש ברוך הוא, רבש"ע! כל נסים שעשית לי ע"י כורש לא היה מוטב לעשותן לי על ידי דניאל ועל ידי אדם צדיק? אף על פי כן "מעי המו עליו".

"My beloved sent out His hand from the hole in the door...." Rabbi Abba bar Kahana said, Being that the nature of a hole in the door is to produce vermin [why is it mentioned here]? But the Assembly of Israel said thus to Hakadosh Baruch Hu: 'Master of the world! All the miracles that You performed for me by the hand of Koresh, would it not have been better to perform them by the hand of Daniel, or some other righteous man? Nevertheless, "my heart was roused for Him."

The opportunity to return to Eretz Yisrael en masse, which signaled the end of the Babylonian exile, was not disqualified because it was spearheaded by an unsavory person such as Koresh. The fact that Hashem did not perform these miracles through righteous people was due to our lack of merits — it was our own fault! But this in no way indicated that we should reject the opportunity to return as being against Hashem's will.

Not only that, Chazal explicitly refer to this series of events as miracles, even though there was seemingly nothing miraculous about them. There was no sounding of the *shofar*, no voice from heaven proclaiming that the redemption had arrived, no unmistakable sign that would silence a skeptic. The opportunity to return to Eretz Yisrael en masse with the consent of the nations of the world is a miracle. It is both a clear sign from heaven that we are *allowed* to return, and a mandate to seize the opportunity — even if Hashem, in His infinite wisdom, chose emissaries who are unsavory to us.

Indeed, Koresh quickly regretted allowing the Jews to leave, and the window of opportunity slammed shut. As the Midrash on Shir Hashirim 5:5 states:

וידי נטפו מור מררים, דגזר כורש ואמר דעבר פרת עבר, דלא עבר לא יעבר. אמר רבי יוחנן כתיב (ישעיה יג:י) "חשך השמש בצאתו", לווי הוה קבל ההוא יומא ולא דנחה. יצא כורש לטייל במדינה וראה המדינה שוממת. אמר מה טיבה של מדינה זו שוממת? איכן הם הזהבים? איכן הם הכספים? אמרי ליה ולאו את הוא דגזרת ואמרת כל יהודאין יפקון ויבנון בית מקדשא? מנהון דהבים ומנהון כספים, הא דסלקין למבנא מקדשא. בההיא שעתא גזר ואמר דעבר פרת עבר דלא עבר לא יעבור.

"And my hands dripped with myrrh ('mor')" — [read it as] *marrorim* (bitterness). For Koresh decreed and said 'Whoever crossed the Euphrates has crossed [and may continue to Eretz Yisrael]. Whoever has not crossed shall not cross.'

Rabbi Yochanan said, It is written (Yeshaya 13:10) *"The sun was darkened when it went out."* If only it would have been dark on that day and the sun didn't rise!

Koresh went out for a stroll in his country and saw the state was desolate. He said, 'Why is this state desolate? Where are the goldsmiths? Where are the silversmiths?' They said to him, 'Isn't it you who decreed and said all the Jews should go out and build the Beis Hamikdash? They are the goldsmiths and silversmiths, who went up to build the Mikdash.'

At that time he decreed and said, 'Whoever crossed the Euphrates has passed. Whoever has not crossed shall not cross.'

Unfortunately, not nearly enough Jews seized the divine opportunity when the window was open. The vast majority of Jews — good frum Jews who go to shul, and study Torah, and run to do *mitzvos* — voluntarily chose to remain in *galus* for all the same reasons they conjure up today. No doubt there were many Torah scholars among them who devised clever rabbinic arguments.

This was no small mistake. Chazal teach that the failure of *galus* Jewry to recognize the opportunity for what it was and seize it caused the second Beis Hamikdash to be destroyed, with all that followed.

This is established by a Mishna in Yoma 66a:

וכבש עשו לו מפני הבבליים שהיו מתלשים בשערו ואומרים לו טול וצא טול וצא.

They made a ramp for it [the שעיר המשתלח, the goat that was sent away on Yom Kippur carrying the sins of the Jewish people] because of the Babylonians, who would tear off its hair and say to it "Carry and go, carry and go."

The Gemara explains:

אמר רבה בר בר חנה לא בבליים היו, אלא אלכסנדריים היו, ומתוך ששונאים את הבבליים היו קורין אותן על שמן.

Rabba bar bar Chana said, They were not Babylonians, but Alexandrians, but since they hated the Babylonians, they called them by that name.

Rashi explains that the Jews of Israel (including the greatest Torah scholars) derisively called anyone who behaved foolishly and inappropriately a Babylonian. The Tosfos Yom Tov on the Mishna adds that this was specifically because they did not move to Eretz Yisrael in the times of Ezra — hundreds of years earlier!

This hatred — which is clearly taken as justified — continued for many more centuries. The Midrash on Shir Hashirim 8:9 states:

רבי זעירא נפיק ליה לשוקא למיזבן מקומא. א"ל לדין דהוא תקיל, תקיל יאות! ואמר ליה לית את אזיל לן מן הכא, בבלייא די חריבון אבהתיה בההיא ענתה. אמר ר' זעירא לית אבהתי כאבהתהון דהדין? על לבית ועדא ושמע קליה דרבי שילא יתיב דריש, אם חומה היא: אילו עלו ישראל חומה מן הגולה לא חרב בית המקדש פעם שנייה. אמר יפה לימדני עם הארץ.

Rabbi Ze'ira went out to the market to buy some goods. He said to the one who was weighing them, "Weigh them properly."

He replied to him, "Won't you get out of here, you Babylonian whose ancestors destroyed [the Beis Hamikdash]?"

Rabbi Ze'ira then said to himself, "Aren't my ancestors just like his?"

He went to a house of meeting [Beis Midrash] and heard the voice of Rabbi Shila sitting and expounding, "'If she is a wall': Had Israel gone up like a wall from the exile, the Beis Hamikdash would not have been destroyed a second time."

He [Rabbi Ze'ira] said, "That am ha'aretz [commoner] taught me well."

Unlike the hypersensitive people of today, who react with outrage and hubris when rebuked for their own glaring sins, Rabbi Ze'eira accepted the stinging retort of a simple shopkeeper that his ancestors were responsible for the destruction of the Beis Hamikdash for remaining in *galus*!

This resentment of Jews in Eretz Yisrael toward their Babylonian brethren — which festered for at least 800 years! — was not limited to commoners. The same Midrash continues:

ריש לקיש כד הוה חמי להון מצמתין בשוקא הוה אמר להון, בדרו גרמיכון! א"ל בעליתכם לא נעשיתם חומה, וכאן באתם לעשות חומה? ר' יוחנן כד הוה חמי להון הוה מקנתר להון. אמר מה נביא מקנתר להון, שנאמר (הושע ט:יז) "ימאסם אלהי כי לא שמעו לו", ואנא לית אנא מקנתר להון.

When Reish Lakish would see them [Babylonians] packed together in the market he would say to them, "Scatter yourselves!" He would say to them, "When you went up you did not become like a wall [come as a group], yet here you come to make a wall?"

When Rabbi Yochanan would see them he would rebuke them. He said, "Just as the prophet rebukes them, as it says (Hoshea 9:17) 'My God rejects them, for they did not listen to Him,' shall I not rebuke them?"

A similar source is found in Yoma 9b:

ריש לקיש הוי סחי בירדנא. אתא רבה בר בר חנה יהב ליה ידא. אמר

ליה אלהא! סנינא לכו, דכתיב (שיר השירים ח:ט) "אם חומה היא נבנה עליה טירת כסף ואם דלת היא נצור עליה לוח ארז", אם עשיתם עצמכם כחומה ועליתם כולכם בימי עזרא נמשלתם ככסף שאין רקב שולט בו. עכשיו שעליתם כדלתות נמשלתם כארז שהרקב שולט בו.

> *Reish Lakish was swimming in the Jordan River. Rabba bar bar Chana extended him a hand. [Reish Lakish refused to take his hand.] He said, 'By God! I hate you, as it is written 'If it is a wall, we will build for it a palace of silver, and if it is a door, we will affix it with boards of cedar' (Shir HaShirim 8:9). Had you made yourselves like a wall and all gone up in the days of Ezra, you would have been compared to silver, which does not rot. Now that you went up like doors [Rashi: like one person opening and another person closing, meaning that the Jews made aliya only partially] you were compared to cedar, which is liable to rot.'*

It must be emphasized that Reish Lakish and Rabbi Yochanan were not rebuking the Babylonians merely for the failure of their ancestors to move to Eretz Yisrael en masse during the period of the second Beis Hamikdash, but for the continued obstinance of their people to remain in *galus*. This is further illustrated by the continuation of the Midrash:

אמר רבי אבא בר כהנא אם ראית ספסלין מלאין בבליין בארץ ישראל צפה לרגלי מלך המשיח. מה טעם? (איכה א:יג) "פרש רשת לרגלי".

> *Rabbi Abba bar Kahana said, If you see benches in Eretz Yisrael filled with Babylonians, look forward to the feet of the King Moshiach. What is the reason? (Eicha 1:13) "He spread out a net for my feet."*

Clearly, not only are the Jewish people expected to return to Eretz Yisrael en masse when given the opportunity, they are sharply rebuked for failing to do so, and in fact are holding back the coming of Moshiach. Were it not for this, it would have been unjustified for anyone, let alone our greatest Talmudic sages, to continue to resent the Babylonians 800 years after their ancestors elected to remain in *galus*.

We should learn from this mistake and accept the rebuke today.

Chazal's presumption that Torah scholars wouldn't stay behind

The Midrash on Shir Hashirim 5:5 cited earlier continues:

דניאל וסיעתו וחבורתו עלו באותה שעה. אמרו מוטב שנאכל סעודת ארץ ישראל ונברך על ארץ ישראל. עזרא וסיעתו וחבורתו לא עלו באותה שעה. ולמה לא עלה באותה שעה? עזרא שהיה צריך לברר תלמודו לפני ברוך בן נריה ויעלה ברוך בן נריה! אלא אמרי ברוך בן נריה אדם גדול וישיש היה, ואפילו בגלקטיקא לא היה יכול להטען.

> *Daniel and his supporters and his group went up [to Eretz Yisrael] at that time. They said, Better that we should eat the meals of Eretz Yisrael and make the blessings over Eretz Yisrael.*
>
> *Ezra and his supporters and his group did not go up at that time. Why did they not go up at that time? Ezra did not because he needed to clarify his learning before Baruch ben Nerya.*
>
> *So Baruch ben Nerya should have gone up!*
>
> *But it is said that Baruch ben Nerya was a heavy man and very old, and couldn't have even been borne in a carriage.*

Chazal take it for granted that everyone who was physically able to travel to Eretz Yisrael — or at least be carried there by others — was expected to go up when Koresh gave them permission. Only Ezra had a temporary exemption to remain in Babylonia to finish learning by his Rebbe, the aged prophet and protégé of Yirmiya from the times of the first Beis Hamikdash, and then he immediately went to Eretz Yisrael.

Chazal do not entertain the notion that they should have stayed behind to continue leading their flock (to nowhere) in the diaspora. The Torah sages were expected to lead their flock back to Jerusalem. Those who chose to stay behind would stay behind without them.

The excuses ring hollow and contradict Chazal

One of the more perverse arguments some people make to remain in *galus* is that they are not worthy of living in Eretz Yisrael. The consequences of sinning in Eretz Yisrael are magnified due to the holiness of the land, and they are afraid they cannot live up to this higher standard.

What humility! What fear of sin! If only such humility and fear of sin were always on display, and not just a self-righteous, ironically arrogant excuse to remain in *galus*.

According to their "logic," Eretz Yisrael should be abandoned to only the saintliest of Jews and those who have no fear of sin at all.

And according to their "logic," one wonders why these people allow themselves to visit Israel for vacations, holidays, and family occasions. Sometimes they even come for extended visits. Why does their fear of sinning in the holy Land of Israel impede them from living in Eretz Yisrael, but not from visiting? Are they so sure they can control themselves for a week, or a summer, or a year?

The wiles of the *yetzer hara* and the human mind are something to behold.

Their argument not only rings hollow, it is contradicted by Chazal. The Midrash on Ruth 2:11 states:

כתוב אחד אומר (תהלים צד:יד) "כי לא יטוש ה' עמו ונחלתו לא יעזוב", וכתוב אחד אומר (שמואל א יב:כב) "כי לא יטוש ה' את עמו בעבור שמו הגדול." א"ר שמואל בר נחמני פעמים שהוא עושה בעבור עמו ונחלתו, ופעמים שהוא עושה בשביל שמו הגדול. א"ר איבי כשישראל זכאין בעבור עמו ונחלתו, וכשאין ישראל זכאין, בעבור שמו הגדול.

ורבנן אמרי בא"י בשביל עמו ונחלתו, בחוצה לארץ, בעבור שמו הגדול, שנאמר (ישעיה מח:יא) "למעני למעני אעשה."

One verse says (Tehillim 94:14) "For Hashem will not abandon His people, and He will not leave His inheritance," and another verse says (Shmuel I 12:22) "For Hashem will not abandon His people, for the sake of His great name."

Rabbi Shmuel bar Nachmani said, Sometimes [He will do it] for the sake of His people and His inheritance, and sometimes for the sake of His great name.

Rabbi Ayvi said, When Israel is meritorious, [He will do it] for the sake of His nation and His inheritance, and when Israel is not meritorious, for the sake of His great name.

The Rabbis said, In Eretz Yisrael [He will do it] for the sake of His nation and His inheritance, and outside the land for the sake of His great name, as it says (Yeshaya 48:11) "For My sake, for My sake I will do it."

The Yefe Anaf explains:

כי העם היושב בה הם נשוא עון וזכותם רב, ולהכי בעבור נחלתו סגי. ואע"ג דשמואל שאמר בעבור שמו הגדול היה בארץ ישראל, מכל מקום שמואל אמר להם כי לא יתיאשו מן הרחמים, כי טוב ה' ועושה חסד בעבור שמו הגדול גם ליושבי חו"ל, וכ"ש שישמע להם בארץ ישראל אף שהם חוטאים.

For the people who dwell in it [the Land of Israel] have their sins borne [by Hashem] and their merit is great. Therefore, "for the sake of His inheritance" is sufficient. And even though Shmuel, who said "for the sake of His great name" was in Eretz Yisrael, nevertheless Shmuel said to them that they should not despair from mercy, for Hashem is good and does kindness for the sake of His great name even for residents of Chutz La'aretz — and certainly He will listen to them in Eretz Yisrael, even when they are sinners.

Eicha Rabba 3:7 states it as clearly as can be:

זכור תזכור. תני ר' חייא משל למלך שיצא למלחמה והיו בניו עמו והיו מקניטין אותו. למחר יצא המלך לבדו ולא היו בניו עמו. אמר המלך

הלואי היו בני עמי ואפילו היו מקניטים אותי. כך המלך זה הקדוש ברוך הוא, בניו אלו ישראל. בשעה שהיו ישראל יוצאין למלחמה היה הקדוש ברוך הוא יוצא עמהם. כיון שהכעיסוהו לא יצא עמהם, וכיון שלא היו ישראל בארץ אמר הלואי היו ישראל עמי ואפילו היו מכעיסים אותי, ואית לן ג' פסוקים (ירמיה ט:א) "מי יתנני במדבר מלון אורחים" "מי יתן עמי עמי כמראש כשהיה במדבר, וכתיב (יחזקאל לו:יז) "בן אדם בית ישראל יושבים על אדמתם וגו'", והדין "זכור תזכור ותשוח עלי נפשי".

"I surely remember" — Rabbi Chiya taught, it can be likened to a king who went out to war, and his sons were with him, and they were provoking him. The following day the king went out alone, and his sons were not with him. The king said, "If only my sons were with me, even if they were provoking me."

Similarly the king [in the parable] is Hakadosh Baruch Hu, and His sons are Israel. At the time Israel would go out to war, Hakadosh Baruch Hu would go out with them. After which they angered Him, He did not go out with them, and after Israel was no longer in the land He said, "If only Israel were with Me, even if they would anger Me."

And there are three verses [that illustrate this idea]: "If only I were in the desert, in a lodge for travelers" (Yirmiya 9:1) — I wish My people were with Me like at first when they were in the desert. And it is written, (Yechezkel 36:17) "Son of man, the house of Israel is dwelling on their land," and this one, (Eicha 3:20) "I surely remember, and my soul is prostrated."

If only *we* wanted to return to Eretz Yisrael, even if we are far from perfect, as much as Hashem wants us to return!

Wicked leadership is not an excuse to abandon the land

Bamidbar Rabba 13:14 states as follows in reference to the sacrifices of the *nesi'im* during the inauguration of the Mishkan, which were replete with symbolic meaning:

אילים חמשה עתודים חמשה כבשים בני שנה חמשה, כנגד חמשה עשר מלכים שהיו מרחבעם ועד צדקיהו שהיו מלך בן מלך. מהם צדיקים גמורים, מהם בינונים, מהם רשעים גמורים.

> *"Five rams, five goats, five lambs one-year-old"*: This corresponds to fifteen kings that were from Rechavam until Tzidkiyahu, who were each a king, the son of a king. Some of them were entirely righteous, some of them were in the middle, some of them were entirely wicked.

The rulership of Eretz Yisrael vacillated back and forth from one extreme to the other, and included many periods when the kings were entirely wicked. There were times when the land was filled with idolatry and other grievous sins, spearheaded by evil, tyrannical kings. Nevertheless, we have no record of the minority of righteous Jews in Eretz Yisrael abandoning the land in favor of safer spiritual pastures, nor is such a notion entertained anywhere by Chazal.

The Gemara in Kesubos 110b takes this point a step further:

ת"ר לעולם ידור אדם בארץ ישראל אפילו בעיר שרובה עובדי כוכבים, ואל ידור בחו"ל ואפילו בעיר שרובה ישראל, שכל הדר בארץ ישראל דומה כמי שיש לו אלוה, וכל הדר בחוצה לארץ דומה כמי שאין לו אלוה, שנא' (ויקרא כה:לח) "לתת לכם את ארץ כנען להיות לכם לאלהים", וכל

שאינו דר בארץ אין לו אלוה? אלא לומר לך כל הדר בחו"ל כאילו עובד עבודת כוכבים, וכן בדוד הוא אומר (שמואל א כו:יט) "כי גרשוני היום מהסתפח בנחלת ה' לאמר לך עבוד אלהים אחרים", וכי מי אמר לו לדוד לך עבוד אלהים אחרים? אלא לומר לך כל הדר בחו"ל כאילו עובד עבודת כוכבים.

The Rabbis taught: One should always dwell in Israel, even in a city that is mostly heathen, and not dwell outside of Israel, even in a city that is mostly Jewish — for anyone who dwells in the Land of Israel is likened to one who has a God, and anyone who dwells outside the land is likened to one who has no God, as it states "To give you the land of Canaan, to be for you a God."

But does anyone who does not dwell in the land not have a God?! Rather, it is coming to tell you that anyone who dwells outside the land is as if he is worshipping idolatry. And so by David it says, (Shmuel I 26:19) "For they have driven me out today from being gathered in the inheritance of Hashem, saying 'go worship other gods.'" Now who told David to go serve other gods? Rather, it is telling you that anyone who dwells outside the land is as if he is worshipping idolatry.

Not only should those in Eretz Yisrael stay in the land even if it is rampant with idolatry, but the Jews outside the land should favor such a living situation over a holy shtetl in *galus*.

It should be noted that this *halachic* Gemara immediately precedes the dispute between Rabbi Ze'eira, who desired to move to Eretz Yisrael, and Rabbi Yehuda. Both agreed that there was an oath not to go up like a wall (en masse, with force), but Rabbi Yehuda took a more extreme position that even individuals from Babylonia should not go up, based on his understanding of the pesukim.

Chazal did not bring this as a *"ma'aseh listor,"* a story to contradict the *halacha* that had just been taught. Rather, it is to illustrate the *halacha* that one is indeed allowed and encouraged to move to Eretz Yisrael, so long as he is not raising an army to force the end of the exile.

One needs a heter to LEAVE Eretz Yisrael

It is not those who wish to move to Eretz Yisrael who need a *halachic* exemption, but those who wish to leave Eretz Yisrael. As Chazal teach in multiple places, it is forbidden to leave Eretz Yisrael for Chutz La'aretz (Gittin 76b, Kiddushin 31b, Avoda Zara 13a, Shevi'is 16b, Rambam Hilchos Melachim 5:9, etc.). Although there are notable exceptions to the rule, this is the starting point.

In our times the rule has completely been turned on its head; the exceptions have been expanded to the extent that the rule is rendered irrelevant. Anyone who wishes to leave Eretz Yisrael for any reason can find a *heter*, assuming he even bothers to seek one. Even in communities where people pride themselves on taking *halachic* stringencies, this one — which is not a stringency, but a *halacha* itself — is virtually ignored. One who declares that he will not leave Eretz Yisrael because it is forbidden by *halacha* is looked upon as a saint or a fool. Doesn't he know that anything and everything is an exception?

The fact that Chazal were extremely hesitant to permit someone to leave Eretz Yisrael underscores what a tremendous *mitzvah* and merit it is to live in Eretz Yisrael — even before Moshiach comes — and Hashem's will for Jews to remain there. Nowhere in the *halachic* discussion do they indicate that oaths have any practical bearing on the matter, nor do they qualify the *halacha* based on whether or not Moshiach has come, or who rules over Eretz Yisrael at a given time.

Additionally, were it prohibited for Jews to move to Eretz Yisrael in numbers great or small before Moshiach comes, Chazal would not have prohibited them from leaving the land once they moved and undoing the presumed sin that they committed.

It is excruciating to leave Eretz Yisrael even if one must do so

Even before the Torah was given, our forefathers found it excruciating to leave the land. For example, in Bereishis 46:3 Hashem told Yaacov not to be afraid to descend to Egypt. Rashi explains:

לפי שהיה מיצר על שנזקק לצאת לחוצה לארץ.

Because he was troubled that he was required to leave to Chutz La'aretz.

Rashi's source, Pirkei D'Rabbi Eliezer 39:1 elaborates:

שמע יעקב על יוסף שהוא חי והיה מהרהר בלבו ואומר איך אעזב ארץ אבותי וארץ מולדתי ואת ארץ ששכינתו של הקדוש ברוך הוא בקרבה, ואלך אל ארץ טמאה, לתוך העבדים בני חם, בארץ שאין יראת שמים ביניהם? אמר לו הקדוש ברוך הוא: יעקב, אל תירא מרדה מצרימה, אנכי אהיה עמך.

Yaacov heard that Yosef was alive, and he thought to himself and said, How can I leave the land of my fathers, and the land of my birthplace, and the land that has the presence of Hakadosh Baruch Hu in its midst, and go to an impure land, among the slaves, the children of Cham, in a land in which there is no fear of Heaven between them?
Hakadosh Baruch Hu said to him, Yaacov, don't be afraid of going down to Egypt; I will be with you.

Settling Eretz Yisrael takes precedence

Jewish law gives paramount importance to supporting the settlement — and resettlement — of Eretz Yisrael, even before Moshiach comes, with no qualifications due to oaths or who rules the land. For example:

1) It is permitted to tell a gentile to write a contract on Shabbos, even though this is normally a rabbinic prohibition, in order for a Jew to purchase a home in Eretz Yisrael. As it states in Bava Kama 80b:

משום ישוב ארץ ישראל לא גזרו ביה רבנן.

For the sake of settling the land of Israel, the rabbis did not make a decree in this case.

2) When one is giving tzedaka, poor relatives take precedence over strangers, and the poor people in one's city take precedence over those in other cities. Then there is the following *halacha*:

ויושבי ארץ ישראל קודמין ליושבי חוצה לארץ.

The inhabitants of the land of Israel come before the inhabitants of Chutz La'aretz.
(Shulchan Aruch Yoreh De'ah 251:3).

This *halacha* actually incentivizes poor people to move to Israel en masse so they can jump to the head of the line. Why would we favor people who violate an oath over the good *galus* Jews who are dutifully waiting for Moshiach? This goes against the principle of לא יהא חוטא נשכר, a sinner should not profit.

3) If one sells his slave outside Eretz Yisrael, he goes free, and the one who purchases him forfeits his money (Gittin 44b).

Even if a Jewish-owned slave flees to Eretz Yisrael, he is not extradited, and his master is told "Sell him here and go, for the sake of settling Eretz Yisrael" (Kesubos 110b).

The Rambam in Hilchos Avadim 8:9 and the Shulchan Aruch Yoreh De'ah 267:84 further codify the *halacha*:

עבד שאמר לעלות לארץ ישראל, כופין את רבו לעלות עמו או ימכור אותו למי שיעלהו שם רצה. האדון לצאת לחוצה לארץ, אינו יכול להוציא את עבדו עד שירצה. ודין זה בכל זמן, אפילו בזמן הזה שהארץ ביד עובדי כוכבים.

If a slave says he wishes to go up to Eretz Yisrael, we force his master to go up with him, or sell him to one who will bring him up. If the master wants to go out to Chutz La'aretz, he is unable to take out his slave unless he consents. This law applies at all times, even in these times, when the land is in the hands of idolaters.

4) Both a husband and a wife can compel the other to move to Eretz Yisrael, and if the other refuses, it is grounds for divorce without penalty (Kesubos 110b). We know how strongly the Torah discourages divorce; they would certainly not make an exception so one or both parties could violate an oath!

5) The Shulach Aruch Yoreh De'ah 228:36 writes:

מי שנדר לעלות לארץ ישראל יש לו התרה כשאר נדרים.

One who took a vow to go up to Eretz Yisrael may have it annulled like other vows.

Normally a vow to perform a *mitzvah* cannot be annulled. The Pischei Teshuva cites the Teshuvos Rashbash Siman 2, who explains that this vow can be annulled because going up to Eretz Yisrael is a preparatory step to performing the *mitzvah* of dwelling in Eretz Yisrael (just as building a succah is a preparatory step to performing the *mitzvah* of dwelling in a succah). Conversely, if one took a vow not to dwell in Eretz Yisrael, he would not be able to have it annulled (aside from exceptional circumstances, as the Rashbash discusses).

This is because living in Eretz Yisrael is a *mitzvah* at all times, one that we should yearn to fulfill and regret missing if we are unable to fulfill it for truly acceptable reasons.

Indeed, the Rashbash explicitly states that going up to live in Eretz Yisrael is a great *mitzvah* that is incumbent upon every individual Jew, applicable at all times, while also acknowledging the "oaths" not to attempt to expedite the end of times or go up with force.

Jewish law clearly encourages people to settle the land of Israel, remain in the land of Israel, and otherwise support the resettlement of the land.

A mitzvah *even during the period of exile*

The Ramban in his critique of the Sefer Hamitzvos of the Rambam, positive commandment four that he says the Rambam forgot to include, writes at length that it is a *mitzvah* in all generations for us to settle Eretz Yisrael. Key excerpts follow:

שנצטווינו לרשת הארץ אשר נתן האל יתעלה לאבותינו לאברהם ליצחק וליעקב ולא נעזבה ביד זולתנו מן האומות או לשממה והוא אמר להם "והורשתם את הארץ וישבתם בה כי לכם נתתי את הארץ לרשת אותה והתנחלתם את הארץ אשר נשבעתי לאבותיכם"... וזו היא שחכמים קורין אותה מלחמת מצות... ואומר אני כי המצוה שחכמים מפליגים בה והוא דירת ארץ ישראל עד שאמרו כתובות (דף ק:) כל היוצא ממנה ודר בחוצה לארץ יהא בעיניך כעובד ע"ז שנאמר כי גרשוני היום מהסתפח בנחלת ה' לאמר לך עבוד אלהים אחרים, וזולת זה הפלגות גדולות שאמרו בה, הכל הוא ממצות עשה הוא שנצטווינו לרשת הארץ לשבת בה, א"כ היא מצות עשה לדורות מתחייב כל אחד ממנו, ואפילו בזמן גלות, כידוע בתלמוד במקומות הרבה. ולשון ספרי מעשה ברבי יהודה בן בתירא ורבי מתיא בן חרש ורבי חנניה בן אחי ר' יהושע ור' נתן שהיו יוצאין חוצה לארץ והגיעו לפלטיא וזכרו את ארץ ישראל וזקפו את עיניהם זלגו דמעותיהן וקרעו בגדיהם וקראו המקרא הזה וירשתה וישבת בה ושמרת לעשות. ואמרו ישיבת ארץ ישראל שקולה כנגד כל המצות.

> *That we are commanded to take possession of the land that the exalted God gave to our forefathers, to Avraham, Yitzchak, and Yaacov, and we should not abandon it to the hands of anyone else from the nations, or to be desolate. And this is as He said to them, "And you shall take possession of the land and settle in it, for to you I have given the land to take possession of it, and you shall take the land as an inheritance that I swore to your forefathers"...And this is what our Sages referred to as*

milchemes mitzvos [a war that is a mitzvah]...

And I say that the mitzvah that our Sages speak exceedingly about, that is residing in Eretz Yisrael, to the point that they said in Kesubos (100b) "Whoever goes out from it and lives in Chutz La'aretz should be in your eyes like one who serves idolatry, as it says (Shmuel I 26:19) 'For they have driven me away today from being gathered in the inheritance of Hashem, saying go serve other gods,'" and many other extraordinary things they said about it — all of it is from this positive commandment that we were commanded to take possession of the land and settle in it.

Hence, this is a positive commandment for the generations that everyone is obligated therefrom, even in a time of exile, as is known from the Talmud in many places.

And the language of the Sifrei: It happened with Rabbi Yehuda ben Beseira, Rabbi Masya ben Charash, Rabbi Chananya the nephew of Rabbi Yehoshua, and Rabbi Yonasan, who were going out to Chutz La'aretz, that they reached Paltom, and they remembered Eretz Yisrael. They lifted their eyes, their tears flowed, they tore their clothing, and read this verse (Devarim 11:31): "And you shall inherit it and settle in it and take care to do all of these laws." And they said, Living in Eretz Yisrael weighs as much as all the mitzvos in the Torah.

Important note: Rabbi Yissachar Shlomo Teichtal, may Hashem avenge his blood, explains in great detail in Eim Habanim Semeicha that the Rambam does not disagree with the Ramban that it is a Torah commandment to settle the Land of Israel. Rather, the Rambam did not include it in the list of 613 commandments because it is an overarching commandment. The disagreement is a technical matter, but in practicality the Rambam and the Ramban agree that we have a *mitzvah* to settle the Land of Israel at all times.

Treasuring cattle more than souls

For all the pious reasons people give for rejecting Eretz Yisrael in favor of *galus*, almost invariably it's about materialism — unjustified materialism. In the end, it isn't a good bargain.

Bamidbar Rabba 22:7 states as follows:

וכן אתה מוצא בבני גד ובני ראובן, שהיו עשירים והיה להם מקנה גדול וחבבו את ממונם וישבו להם חוץ מארץ ישראל, לפיכך גלו תחלה מכל השבטים, שנאמר (דברי הימים א ה:כו) "ויגלם לראובני ולגדי ולחצי שבט מנשה" ומי גרם להם? על שהפרישו עצמם מן אחיהם בשביל קנינם. מנין? ממה שכתוב בתורה ומקנה רב היה לבני ראובן וגו'.

And so you find by the sons of Gad and the sons of Reuven, who were wealthy and they had a great amount of cattle, and they treasured their money, and they settled for themselves outside the Land of Israel. Therefore they were exiled first of all the tribes, as it says (Divrei Hayamim I 5:26) "And he exiled those from Reuven, Gad, and half the tribe of Menashe." What caused this for them? That they separated themselves from their brothers for the sake of their possessions. From where do we know this? From what is written in the Torah, "And there was much cattle for the sons of Reuven, etc."

The Midrash continues in 22:9:

"לב חכם לימינו" (קהלת י:ב) זה משה. "ולב כסיל לשמאלו", אלו בני ראובן ובני גד, שעשו את העיקר טפל ואת הטפל עיקר, שחיבבו את ממונם יותר מן הנפשות, שהן אומרים למשה גדרת צאן נבנה למקננו פה וערים לטפנו. אמר להם משה אינה כלום! אלא עשו את העיקר עיקר. תחלה בנו לכם ערים לטפכם, ואחר כך וגדרת לצנאכם. הוי לב חכם לימינו, זה משה, ולב כסיל לשמאלו, אלו בני ראובן ובני גד. אמר

להם הקב"ה אתם חיבבתם את מקניכם יותר מן הנפשות, חייכם אין בו ברכה עליהם. נאמר (משלי כ:כא) "נחלה מבוהלת בראשונה ואחריתה לא תבורך", וכה"א (שם כג:ד) "אל תיגע להעשיר מבינתך חדל", ואיזה הוא עשיר? השמח בחלקו, שנאמר (תהלים קכח:ב) "יגיע כפיך כי תאכל אשריך וטוב לך".

"The heart of a wise person is to his right" (Koheles 10:2) — This is Moshe. *"And the heart of a fool is to his left"* — These are the sons of Reuven and the sons of Gad, who made the primary secondary and the secondary primary, for they treasured their money more than souls, for they said to Moshe *"We will build sheep stables for our cattle here and cities for our small children."*

Moshe said to them, *"That is nothing. Rather, make the primary primary. First 'build for yourselves cities for your small children', and after that 'stables for your sheep'."*

Thus *"the heart of a wise person is to his right"* is Moshe, and *"the heart of a fool is to his left"* are the sons of Reuven and the sons of Gad.

Hakadosh Baruch Hu said to them, *"You treasured your cattle more than souls? By your lives! No blessing will be upon them."* It says (Mishlei 20:21) *"An inheritance acquired in haste at first will not be blessed in the end"* and similarly it says (Mishlei 23:4) *"Don't toil to become wealthy; from your own understanding, desist."* And who is wealthy? One who is happy with his lot, as it says (Tehillim 128:2) *"When you consume the toil of your palms, you will be praised and it will be good for you."*

They prioritized their money over their own children, and they lost it all as a direct result. In the end, they learned their lesson the hard way. Koheles Rabba 4:6 states as follows:

רבי יצחק פתר קרייא בשבט גד ושבט ראובן, שבאו לארץ ישראל וראו כמה בית זרע יש בה, כמה בית נטע יש בה. אמרו טוב מלא נחת בארץ ישראל ממלא חפנים בעבר הירדן, וחזרו ואמרו מה, לא אנן גרמינן לן? לא אמרין אנן יותן את הארץ הזאת לעבדיך.

Rabbi Yitzchak interpreted the verse in reference to the tribe of Gad and the tribe of Reuven, for they came to Eretz Yisrael and saw how many sown fields and plantations were there. They said, "A handful with pleasantness is better" in Eretz Yisrael "than two handfuls on the other side of the Jordan."

They went back and said, "Didn't we cause this to ourselves? Didn't we say 'Let this land be given to your servants?'"

We should learn from their mistake and not have to learn the hard way yet again, God forbid.

Moshiach comes after the ingathering

It is crystal clear from a mountain of Torah sources that not only is it permitted for Jews to return en masse before Moshiach comes... and not only is it desirable...but it is inevitable.

Contemporary misconceptions notwithstanding, this is not even a controversial point. Chazal took it for granted that the ingathering of the exiles would already take place (despite being incomplete) before Moshiach comes — and that this was a good thing.

Here is a sample of clear sources to this effect. Shir Hashirim Rabba 2:13:

"התאנה חנטה פניה", אמר רבי חייא בר אבא סמוך לימות המשיח דבר גדול בא לעולם והרשעים כלים, והגפנים סמדר נתנו ריח, אלו הנשארים ועליהם נאמר (ישעיה ד:ג) "והיה הנשאר בציון והנותר בירושלם."

"The fig tree puts forth her green figs." Rabbi Hiyya bar Abba said: Shortly before the days of the Moshiach a great epidemic will come upon the world and the wicked will vanish. "And the vines in blossom give forth their fragrance": this refers to the survivors, spoken of in the verse (Yeshaya 4:3) "And it shall come to pass, that he that is left in Zion, and he that remains in Jerusalem."

Clearly there is a large contingent of Jews in Jerusalem before Moshiach comes, and they merit to be saved from the epidemic for this very reason.

Shir Hashirim Rabba 4:16 (also found in Bamidbar Rabba 13:2):

מה מקיים ר' אלעזר קרא דין "עורי צפון ובואי תימן?" לכשיתעוררו

הגליות הנתונות בצפון ויבאו יחנו בדרום, היך מה דאת אמר (ירמיה לא:ח) "הנני מביא אותם מארץ צפון וקבצתים מירכתי ארץ", לכשיתעורר גוג ומגוג שנתון בצפון ויבא ויפול בדרום, היך מה דאת אמר (יחזקאל לט:ב) "ושבבתיך וששאתיך והעליתיך", לכשיתעורר מלך המשיח שנתון בצפון ויבא ויבנה בית המקדש שנתון בדרום, היך מה דאת אמר (ישעיה מא:כה) "העירותי מצפון ויאת".

How does Rabbi Elazar explain this verse? "Awaken, O north, and come, O south." When the exiles that are found in the north will stir and come and encamp in the south.

[Additionally] as it says, (Yirmiya 31:8) "Behold, I am bringing them from the land of the north, and gather them from the ends of the earth." When Gog Umagog, who are found in the north, will stir and come, and will fall in the south.

[Additionally] as it says, (Yechezkel 39:2) "And I will turn you back, and carry you, and bring you up [from the ends of the north and bring you upon the mountains of Israel]." When the King Moshiach, who is found in the north, will stir and come and build the Beis Hamikdash, which is found in the south. This is as it says, (Yeshaya 41:25) "I have roused him from the north, and he has come."

The Yefe Kol notes:

מזה נראה כי מתחלה יהיה קבוץ גליות, ואח"ז יבוא מלך המשיח. והכי משמע בפ"ב דמגילה, שתקנו תקע בשופר מתחלה על קבוץ גליות, ואחר זה שאר הברכות עד בונה ירושלים, ע"ש ושים עינך היטב פה על סדור הישועה אשר עליה אנחנו מצפיה.

From here it appears that at first there will be the ingathering of the exiles, after which Moshiach will come. This is also implied in the second chapter of Megilla, that Chazal instituted [the blessing] "Blow the shofar" first for the ingathering of the exiles, and after that the other blessings until "Build Jerusalem," see there. Pay careful attention here to the order of the salvation that we are anticipating.

The Midrash Tanchuma (Buber edition) Noach 17 (also found in the Yalkut Shimoni 888:31 on Tehillim) has a similar teaching:

אמר רבי שמואל בר נחמני מסורת אגדה היא שאין ירושלים נבנית עד

שיתכנסו הגליות. ואם יאמר לך אדם שנבנית ולא נתכנסו הגליות אל תאמין שנאמר בונה ירושלים ה' ואחר כך נדחי ישראל יכנס.

Rabbi Shmuel bar Nachmani said, It is an Aggadic tradition that Jerusalem will not be built until the exiles are brought in. And if someone will say to you that it was built and the exiles were not brought in, do not believe him, as it says, "Hashem builds Jerusalem" and after that "He brings in the dispersed of Israel."

The Malbim on Yeshaya 49:12 writes:

"הנה אלה", פה מתחיל ענין חדש רוצה לצייר כי קיבוץ גלויות יוקדם לבנין ציון, וכי בעת תתקבץ הגולה מארבע רוחות עוד תהיה ירושלים שממה.

"Behold, these [are coming from afar, these from the north and the west, and these from the land of Sinim.]" Here begins a new matter. He wants to illustrate that the ingathering of the exiles precedes the building of Zion, and at the time the exiles are gathered from the four directions, Jerusalem will still be desolate.

The Malbim makes a similar comment on Yeshaya 62:11.

The Gemara in Perek Chelek of Sanhedrin gives numerous signs that the redemption is imminent, with the following appearing on page 98a:

ואמר רבי אבא אין לך קץ מגולה מזה שנאמר (יחזקאל לו:ח) "ואתם הרי ישראל ענפכם תתנו ופריכם תשאו לעמי ישראל וגו'."

And Rabbi Abba said, There is no more revealed sign of the end of days than this, as it says (Yechezkel 36:8) "And you, mountains of Israel, shall give forth your branches and bear your fruit for my people, Israel, [for they are coming soon.]"

Rashi explains:

כשתתן ארץ ישראל פריה בעין יפה אז יקרב הקץ ואין לך קץ מגולה יותר.

When Eretz Yisrael gives forth its fruit generously, then the end of days is near, and there is no sign of the end that is more revealed.

Who, pray tell, are these abundant fruits for, if not for the Jews who return in abundant numbers to enjoy them?

The Gemara in Megilla, referenced by the Yefe Kol above, explains the order of the blessings in Shemoneh Esrei. The relevant section teaches:

ומה ראו לומר קיבוץ גליות לאחר ברכת השנים? דכתיב (יחזקאל לו:ח) "ואתם הרי ישראל ענפכם תתנו ופריכם תשאו לעמי ישראל כי קרבו לבוא", וכיון שנתקבצו גליות נעשה דין ברשעים, שנאמר (ישעיהו א:כה) "ואשיבה ידי עליך ואצרוף כבור סיגיך" וכתיב (ישעיהו א:כו) "ואשיבה שופטיך כבראשונה", וכיון שנעשה דין מן הרשעים כלו הפושעים וכולל זדים עמהם, שנאמר (ישעיהו א:כח) "ושבר פושעים וחטאים יחדיו יכלו", וכיון שכלו הפושעים מתרוממת קרן צדיקים, דכתיב (תהלים עה:יא) "וכל קרני רשעים אגדע תרוממנה קרנות צדיק." והיכן מתרוממת קרנם? בירושלים, שנאמר (תהלים קכב:ו) "שאלו שלום ירושלם ישליו אוהביך", וכיון שנבנית ירושלים בא דוד, שנאמר (הושע ג:ה) "אחר ישובו בני ישראל ובקשו את ה' אלהיהם ואת דוד מלכם."

And what did they [the Anshei Knesses Hagedolah, who arranged the Shemoneh Esrei] see to say [the blessing regarding] the ingathering of the exiles following the blessing for [the prosperity of] the years? As it is written, (Yechezkel 36:8) "And you, mountains of Israel, shall give forth your branches and bear your fruit for my people, Israel, [for they are coming soon.]"

Once the exiles have been gathered, judgment will be done with the wicked, as it says, (Yeshaya 1:25) "And I will turn My hand against you, and I will purge away your dross as with lye," and it is written, (Yeshaya 1:26) "And I will restore your judges like at first."

Once judgment is done with the wicked, the rebellious people will be eradicated, with the willful sinners among them, as it says, (Yeshaya 1:28) "And the destruction of the rebellious ones and the sinners will be together, [those who forsake Hashem] will be eradicated."

Once the rebellious ones are eradicated, the horn of the righteous will be raised, as it is written, (Tehillim 75:11) "And I will cut off all the horns of the wicked; the horns of the righteous shall be raised."

And where will their horns be raised? In Jerusalem, as it says,

(Tehillim 122:6) "Ask [Hashem] for the peace of Jerusalem; those who love you shall be in tranquility."

Once Jerusalem is built, David comes, as it says, (Hoshea 3:5) "Afterward the Jewish people will return and seek Hashem, their God, and David, their king."

Abudarham (Shemoneh Esrei 91) quotes the Riva, a student of Rashi, who elaborates:

ודע כי כל ברכה הקודמת לחברתה מעולה ממנה, והערך אליה גדול מאשר לאחריה. לכן תחלה חונן הדעת, שאם אין דעת אין תשובה, כי לא ידע בין טוב לרע, וכן אם לא ישוב מה תועיל לו סליחת עוונת? הרי הוא חוטא ועושה עון בכל יום! ואם אין סליחת עוונת לא יסורו אויביו וצרותיו, כד"א הוי אשור שבט אפי. ומה תועיל לו בריאותו אם ירדפוהו שונאיו? ומה תועלת בעשרו אם הוא חולה ומעונה? הא למדת שגדולה סליחה מן הפרנסה בשלש מעלות וקנין דעת בחמש.

לכן ראוי לרדוף אחריהם כפי מעלתם, וכל ההולך פרסה אחת כדי לקנות סחורה, הרי הוא חייב לילך ששה פרסאות ללמוד תורה, וכל הסובל עמל ועלבון נפש כדי שלא ינזק בממונו חייב לסבול כפלים כדי שלא יחטא, ואם הוא בעל תשובה כפלים פעמים.

וכן תחלת הגאולה, קבוץ גליות ובהתקבצם ימנו שופטים להשמיד הרשעים, ובכן צדיקים יראו וישמחו, ותשכון שכינה בישראל, ואז בן דוד בא, ולמדת שקבוץ גליות קודם לצמח דוד בדברים רבים. עד כאן דבריו.

And know that every blessing that precedes its fellow is more exalted than it, and its value is greater than that which follows it. Therefore, first is "Who graces us with knowledge," for if there is no knowledge there can be no repentance, for one will not know the difference between good and evil.

Similarly, if one does not repent, what good is the pardon of his sins, for he will sin and commit crimes every day. And if his sins are not pardoned, his enemies and troublemakers will not turn away, as it says "Ho, Assyria, the rod of My anger."

And what good is his health if those who hate him will pursue him, and what good is his wealth if he is sick and suffering?

We learn from here that forgiveness is greater than one's livelihood by three levels [for this blessing precedes the other by three], and the acquisition of knowledge is greater by five levels.

Therefore it is appropriate to pursue them according to their levels, *and one who would travel a parasang to acquire merchandise is obligated to travel six parasangs to learn Torah. And those who would tolerate toil and humiliation so their money would not be harmed are obligated to tolerate double this in order not to sin. And if he is a sinner who repented, he must tolerate this many times over.*

Similarly, [according to the order of the blessings,] the beginning of the redemption is the ingathering of the exiles, and after they gather they will appoint judges to destroy the wicked, and then the righteous will see and rejoice, and then Hashem's presence will settle in Israel, and then [Moshiach] the son of David will come. This teaches that the ingathering of the exiles precedes the blossoming of David with many things. Until here are his [the Riva's] words.

This source alone — about which there is no dispute — is clear enough to end any debate on the matter. Jews who *daven* three times a day for the redemption, but refuse to return to Eretz Yisrael before Moshiach comes, are clueless about what they are asking for, or belying their own prayers.

Either way, their ignorance or intransigence is delaying the redemption, for there is an active role they must play in the fulfillment of these prayers.

What good is it if Hashem says yes to the beginning of the redemption by allowing the ingathering of the exiles, but vast numbers of Jews "piously" choose to remain in *galus*? This can only provoke anger, God forbid.

Hashem's promise is fulfilled even if we return on our own

Radak on Tehillim 146:3 further debunks the excuses of those who are waiting for open miracles or Moshiach to pick them up in a limousine before recognizing that Hashem already said yes:

"אל תבטחו". על הדרך שאמר ירמיה ומה' יסור לבו, אלא אם יבטח באדם ישים העיקר האל יתברך שיתן בלב האדם הנדיב בעזרו, וכפל הענין במלות שונות.
"שאין לו תשועה". שאם לא ברצון האל, אין ביד האדם להושיע חבירו מצרתו, כי לה' לבדו התשועה, והוא יסובבנה על יד בני אדם, כמו שסיבב תשועת גלות בבל על ידי כורש, וכן לעתיד יסבב גאולת ישראל על ידי מלכי הגוים, שיעור את רוחם לשלחם, כמו שכתוב והביאו את כל אחיכם מכל הגוים מנחה לה', וזה יהיה לפי שבטחו ישראל בגלותם באל ית' לבדו.

"Do not trust [in the wealthy and powerful, in human beings who cannot save]." This is in line with what Yirmiya said (17:5) "And he turns his heart away from Hashem." Instead, if he trusts in a person, he should place the primary trust on Hashem that He will put it in the heart of the wealthy and powerful person to help him. The verse repeated this idea in different words.

"For he cannot save": For if not for the will of God, a person has no ability to save his fellow from his trouble, for salvation belongs only to Hashem, and He will bring it about through people — just as He brought about the salvation of the Babylonian exiles through the hands of Koresh. And so in the future He will bring about the redemption of Israel through the hands of the kings of the nations, in that He will arouse their spirits to send them out, as it is written, "And they will bring all your brothers from all the nations as a gift-offering to Hashem," and this will be because Israel in their exile trusted in Hashem alone.

As we saw earlier, the fact that the ingathering of the exiles was initiated by the "good graces" of the nations of the world, and spearheaded by unsavory people, does not in any way disqualify it from being Hashem's will, the authentic redemption process, and the answer to our prayers. On the contrary, we were clearly foretold that it could and even would happen this way.

Radak on Tehillim 108:5 makes an even more startling comment:

במזמור אחד אמר כי גדול עד שמים, שאמרו דוד על עצמו, וזהו שאמר על ישועת ישראל אמר מעל שמים, כי החסד יותר גדול, שיוציא עם אחד מעמים רבים אע"פ שנשקעו בגלות, והוא יוציאם מתחת ידם, ולא עוד אלא שהם עצמם יביאום אל ארץ ישראל בכבוד גדול בצבים ובפרדים ובכרכרות. זה החסד הוא גדול עד מאד שראוי לומר עליו גדול מעל שמים.

ואמר ועד שחקים אמיתך, ולא אמר מעל שחקים, כמו שאמר על חסד מעל שמים, לפי שאמת אינו דבר יתר, אלא דבר הראוי לו לעשות, זה כי כן הבטיחנו על כל פנים יגאלנו, ומה שהבטיח לנו ראוי לקיים דברו, וזהו אמת. ואם נצא בעצמינו דברו יהיה קיים, אבל שנבא בכבוד גדול עד שיהיה לנו מה שנאמר והיו מלכים אומניך וגו' ושאר הנחמות הכתובות עלינו, זהו החסד הגדול.

ואם תאמר גם זה הוא אמת כיון שהבטיחנו בו, יתכן לפרש כי לא הבטיחנו בזה הדבר גדול אלא אם כן נהיה זכאים, אבל גאולתינו על כל פנים תהיה בזמנה, בין זכאים בין חייבים, אלא שאם נהיה זכאים יחיש עתה.

In one psalm it says "For [Your kindness] is great up to the heavens," for David said this regarding himself. In this one, which he said regarding the salvation of Israel, he said "above the heavens," for the kindness is even greater in that He is taking out a people from within many peoples, that even though they became submerged in the exile He will take them out from under their hands. Not only that, they themselves [the nations of the world] will bring them to Eretz Yisrael with great honor, with chariots, mules, and joyous dancing (Yeshaya 66:20). This kindness is extremely great, for which it is worthy to say "it is great above the heavens."

He further said "and Your truthfulness is up to the heavens," and he did not say "above the heavens" as he said about [Hashem's] kindness "above the heavens," because truth is not something that can be above and beyond, but only that which is appropriate for Him to do. This is because He promised us that He will redeem us no matter what, and being that He promised this to us, it is appropriate for Him to fulfill His word. This is trustworthiness.

If we go out on our own, His word is fulfilled. However, for us to come with great honor, to the extent that what is said, "And kings will tend to your children, etc." (Yeshaya 49:23) and the rest of the consolations that are written about us — that is the great kindness.

And if you will say, that too is truth since He promised it to us, it is plausible to explain that He did not promise us this great thing unless we merit it, but our redemption will happen no matter what in its time, whether we are meritorious or guilty. But if we are meritorious, He will hasten its time.

Radak states explicitly that the redemption does not have to come with great fanfare. If the Jews return to Eretz Yisrael on their own (which can only occur if Hashem allows it to happen), it constitutes the fulfillment of Hashem's promise to bring us back to Eretz Yisrael.

Not only is it not prohibited for us to leave *galus* before Moshiach comes, and not only is it not discouraged, but if we take advantage of the opportunity that Hashem gives us, it is the fulfillment of Hashem's promise to redeem us, and His trustworthiness up to the heavens.

How can we not take advantage of the opportunity that Hashem gives us?

Returning to good includes returning to Eretz Yisrael

Indeed, yearning for this opportunity and seizing it when Hashem gives it to us are critical components of the redemption process. As it says in Hoshea 3:5:

אחר ישבו בני ישראל ובקשו את ה' אלהיהם ואת דויד מלכם ופחדו אל ה' ואל טובו באחרית הימים.

Afterward the Jewish people will return and seek Hashem, their God, and David, their king, and they will yearn with fear after Hashem and His goodness at the end of days.

Rashi writes:

תנא משום ר"ש בן יוחאי בג' דברים מאסו בני ישראל בימי רחבעם: במלכות שמים, ובמלכות בית דוד, ובבית המקדש, הה"ד (מלכים א יב:טז) "אין לנו חלק בדוד", כמשמעו, "לאהליך ישראל" אל תקרי לאהליך, אלא לאלהיך, "ראה ביתך דוד", זה בית המקדש. אמר רבי שמעון בן מנסיא אין מראין סימן טוב לישראל עד שיחזרו ויבקשו שלשתן. "אחר ישובו בני ישראל ובקשו את ה'", זו מלכות שמים, "ואת דוד מלכם", כמשמעו, "ופחדו אל ה' ואל טובו", זה בית המקדש, כד"א "ההר הטוב הזה."

They taught in the name of Rabbi Shimon bar Yochai: The Jewish people rejected three things in the days of Rechavam: the kingdom of heaven, the kingdom of the house of David, and the Beis Hamikdash. This is as it says (Melachim I 12:16) "We have no portion in David" — as literally stated; "To your tents, Israel!" Don't read it as "to your tents" but [with two letters transposed] "to your gods." "See now your house, David": This is the Beis Hamikdash.

Rabbi Shimon ben Menasya said, No good sign will be shown to Israel until they return and seek these three things. "Afterward the Jewish people will return and seek Hashem" — this is the kingdom of heaven; "and David, their king" — as literally stated; "and they will yearn with fear after Hashem and His goodness" — this is the Beis Hamikdash, as it says (Devarim 3:25) "on this good mountain."

Metzudas David states clearly that the return of the Jewish people en masse to Eretz Yisrael will precede the coming of Moshiach:

"אחר" ר"ל אחר ימים רבים ישובו בני ישראל אל ארצם, ואז יבקשו את ה' לשאול ממנו צרכם, כי ישוב וישרה שכינתו ביניהם.
"ואת דוד מלכם" וגם יבקשו את מלך המשיח הבא מזרע דוד, ומעמו יבקשו שאלתם כי הוא ימשול בהם, ולא ימלוך בהם עוד מלך ישראל משבט אחר, לא כמו מאז שמלך עליהם ירבעם ושאר מלכי אפרים.

"Afterward" — This means to say that after many days the Jewish people will return to their land, and then they will seek Hashem to ask from Him their needs, for He will return and settle His presence among them.

"And David, their king" — They will also seek the king Moshiach who comes from the descendants of David, and they will ask him to rule over them, and that no longer should a Jewish king rule over them from a different tribe, unlike back then when Yaravam and the other kings of Ephraim ruled over them.

Yeshaya 21:11-12 is a short prophecy about the end of the exile period, specifically the end of *galus Edom*. Rav Yosef Kara comments on 21:12:

אם רצונכם שתהיו נגאלים בקשו רחמים מלפני ושובו מן הגלות ואתיו לכם ושובו בגבולכם.

If you want to be redeemed, ask for mercy from before Me and return from the exile, and you will come and return in your borders.

This clearly indicates a proactive approach, both spiritually and physically, and not passively waiting in *galus* for Moshiach to chauffeur us back to Eretz Yisrael.

The Gemara in Sanhedrin 97b teaches that repentance (literally returning) is the only thing holding back the redemption:

אמר רב כלו כל הקיצין ואין הדבר תלוי אלא בתשובה ומעשים טובים. ושמואל אמר דיו לאבל שיעמוד באבלו. כתנאי ר' אליעזר אומר אם ישראל עושין תשובה נגאלין, ואם לאו אין נגאלין. אמר ליה רבי יהושע אם אין עושין תשובה אין נגאלין? אלא הקב"ה מעמיד להן מלך שגזרותיו קשות כהמן וישראל עושין תשובה ומחזירן למוטב.

Rav said, All the ends of days [that are required for the redemption to occur] are finished, and the matter depends only on repentance and good deeds. Shmuel said, It is enough for the mourner that he stands in his days of mourning.

This follows a dispute among the Tannaim. Rabbi Eliezer said, If Israel repents, they will be redeemed, and if not, they will not be redeemed. Rabbi Yehoshua said to him, If they do not repent they will not be redeemed?! Rather, Hakadosh Baruch Hu will stand up for them a king whose decrees are harsh like Haman, and Israel will repent and they will be returned to goodness.

The Gemara continues with Rabbi Eliezer and Rabbi Yehoshua exchanging proofs from Tanach for their positions. Ultimately Rabbi Yehoshua causes Rabbi Eliezer to become quiet.

Either way, it is clear that some measure of repentance is required for the redemption to occur.

The only dispute is how much the suffering of exile and the passage of time in mourning can compensate for an incomplete repentance, and whether Hashem will force the issue if the Jews are not inspired to repent on their own.

The Ben Yehoyada (more famously known as the Ben Ish Chai) offers a remarkable explanation of this Gemara:

אי נמי יובן בס"ד דארץ ישראל נקראת בשם 'אילה' [46] שהיא ממהרת לבשל פרותיה, וגם אילה סוד לאה, וגם מאיר בה שם א"ל ושם י-ה, וחוץ לארץ נקראת בשם 'אמה' [46] והחשבון שוה זה לעומת זה, ולזה אמר מחזירן למוטב, שיעשו תשובה ויחזרו לארץ ישראל שהיא 'מ"ו טב' טב דאילה מספרה מ"ו, ואמה מספרה מ"ו, אך חוץ לארץ 'מו ביש', וארץ ישראל 'מו טב'.

Alternatively, this can be understood, with the help of heaven, that Eretz Yisrael is called by the name "Ayala" [doe, with the numerical value of 46], for it is quick to ripen its fruit, and "Ayala" also contains the secret of Leah [a Kabbalistic concept], and the names Kel and Kah also shine in it [the word Ayala is formed from the same letters]. Chutz La'aretz is called by the name "Ama" [maidservant, with the numerical value of 46], and the numerical values are equal to one another.

It is for this that it says "machaziran lamutav" [they will be returned to goodness] — that they will repent and return to Eretz Yisrael, which is spelled "Mem Vav [46] Tet Vet." [This refers to] the good that is "Ayala" [Eretz Yisrael], whose numerical value is 46. "Ama" also has the numerical value of 46, except that Chutz La'aretz is "the bad 46," and Eretz Yisrael is "the good 46."

Leaving aside the Kabbalistic concepts, which are beyond me, the Ben Yehoyada addresses the statement in the Gemara that the Jewish people will repent and they will be returned to goodness, which seems to be redundant. He explains that the *teshuva* refers to physically returning to Eretz Yisrael, which will be accompanied by a spiritual return. These together are necessary developments that will usher the redemption.

Before Moshiach comes.

If necessary, this will be instigated by a ruler who issues wicked decrees like Haman. We have no shortage of candidates inside Israel and around the world who qualify for that position.

Incomplete joy precedes Moshiach

Shir Hashirim Rabba 1:4 states:

למטרונה שהלך המלך בעלה ובניה וחתניה למדינת הים, ובאו ואמרו לה באו בניך! אמרה מה איכפת לי? תשמחנה כלותי. כיון שבאו חתניה אמרו לה באו חתניך! אמרה מה איכפת לי? תשמחנה בנותי. אמרו לה בא המלך בעליך! אמרה האי חדוותא שלימה, חדו על חדו. כך לעתיד לבא באין הנביאים ואומרים לירושלים (ישעיה ס:ד) "בניך מרחוק יבואו", והיא אומרת להם מה איכפת לי? "ובנותיך על צד תאמנה", אמרה מה איכפת לי? כיון שאמרו לה (זכריה ט:ט) "הנה מלכך יבא לך צדיק ונושע", אמרה הא חדוותא שלימה, דכתיב (שם) "גילי מאד בת ציון", וכתיב (שם ב:יד) "רני ושמחי בת ציון" באותה שעה היא אומרת (ישעיה סא:י) "שוש אשיש בה' תגל נפשי באלהי".

> This can be likened to a matron whose husband the king, and her sons and sons-in-law, went to a distant land. They came and told her, "Your children have come back." She said, "What do I care? Let my daughters-in-law rejoice." When her sons-in-law came back, they said to her, "Your sons-in-law have come back." She said, "What do I care? Let my daughters rejoice." They said to her, "The king, your husband, has come back." She said, "This is complete joy, joy upon joy."
>
> Similarly in the coming future, the prophets will come and say to Jerusalem, "Your children have come back from a distant place (Yeshaya 60:4)" and she will say to them, "What do I care?" [They said,] "And your daughters carried like young children." She said, "What do I care?" Whereupon they said to her, "Behold your king is coming to you, righteous and victorious" (Zecharya 9:5) she said, "This is complete joy, as it is written "Rejoice greatly, daughter of Zion," and it is written, (Zecharya 2:14) "Shout and celebrate, daughter of Zion." At that time

she says, (Yeshaya 61:10) "I will surely rejoice in Hashem, my soul will celebrate in my God."

This Midrash too clearly indicates that the mass return of Jews to Eretz Yisrael is an inevitable step in the redemption process, but only a precursor to the actual redemption. The intermediary stage, before Moshiach takes over the rulership of Eretz Yisrael, has troubles and incomplete joy — but this should not deter the Jewish people from returning as indicated.

The stragglers wait for Moshiach

Shir Hashirim Rabba 4:8 states:

"תשורי מראש אמנה" אמר רבי חוניא בשם ר' יוסטא עתידות הגליות מניעות עד טיורוס מונוס ואומרים שירה, ועתידים אומות העולם להביא אותה סרדיוטות למלך המשיח....

"Gaze from the top of Amana" — Rabbi Chunya said in the name of Rabbi Yosta, The exiles are destined to reach Mount Amana and say a song, and the nations of the world are destined to bring them like nobles to the King Moshiach....

The Jews who remain in *galus* until Moshiach comes are the stragglers, and likely those who do not know that they are Jewish. Although the nations will later bring them as tribute to Moshiach, the Jews who should have known better and were left behind by their own choosing will surely be ashamed.

In any case, here too it is clear that Moshiach does not come specifically to bring the masses of Jews out of *galus*, but to take over the leadership of the masses of Jews who rightly returned to Eretz Yisrael before he arrived.

Mitzvos *without reward in* galus

Shir Hashirim Rabba 1:6 states:

רבי חייא בשם רבי יוחנן אמרה כנסת ישראל לפני הקדוש ברוך הוא, רבונו של עולם, על שלא שמרתי חלה אחת כתקנה בארץ ישראל, הריני משמרת שתי חלות בסוריא. סבורה הייתי שאני מקבלת שכר על שתים, ואיני מקבלת שכר אלא על אחת. רבי אבא בשם רבי יוחנן אמרה כנסת ישראל לפני הקדוש ברוך הוא, על שלא שמרתי יום טוב אחד כתקונו בארץ ישראל, הריני משמרת שני ימים טובים של גליות בחוצה לארץ. סבורה הייתי שאקבל שכר על שניהם, ואיני מקבלת שכר אלא על אחד. רבי יוחנן הוה קרי עליהון (יחזקאל כ:כה) "וגם אני נתתי להם חקים לא טובים."

Rabbi Chiya said in the name of Rabbi Yochanan, The assembly of Israel said before Hakadosh Baruch Hu, "Master of the world! Because I did not observe [the mitzvah of] one Challah properly in Eretz Yisrael, behold I am [separating] two Challah portions in Syria. I thought I would receive reward for both of them, but I only receive reward for one."

Rabbi Abba said in the name of Rabbi Yochanan, The assembly of Israel said before Hakadosh Baruch Hu, "Because I did not keep one day of Yom Tov properly in Eretz Yisrael, behold I am keeping two days of Yom Tov of the exiles in Chutz La'aretz. I thought I would receive reward for both of them, but I only receive reward for one."

Rabbi Yochanan would read in reference to them, (Yechezkel 20:25) "And I too gave them laws that weren't good."

This is a remarkable source. Jews in *galus* are obligated to keep a second day of Yom Tov and other additional observances, but they get no extra reward for it whatsoever. Chazal view it as nothing more than a negative consequence of being in *galus*, more obligations with nothing to show for it, in return for not properly observing the *mitzvos* in Eretz Yisrael, where we are supposed to be.

Indeed, this aligns with the principle we cited earlier, לא יהא חוטא נשכר, a sinner should not profit. Jews do not profit spiritually from being in *galus*.

Eretz Yisrael is not a cemetery, but our homeland

Unfortunately, many *galus* Jews recognize the spiritual benefits of Eretz Yisrael, but don't want to receive these benefits during their lifetime, only after they die. Bereishis Rabba 96:5 has a response to this:

ולמה כל האבות תובעין ומחבבין קבורת ארץ ישראל? א"ר אלעזר דברים בגו. רבי יהושע בן לוי אמר מהו דברים בגו? (תהלים קיז:ט) "אתהלך לפני ה' בארצות החיים." אמרו רבותינו שני דברים בשם רבי חלבו, למה האבות מחבבין קבורת ארץ ישראל? שמתי ארץ ישראל חיים תחלה בימות המשיח ואוכלין שנות המשיח. ר' חנינא אמר מי שמת בחוץ לארץ ונקבר שם, שתי מיתות יש בידו, שכך כתיב (ירמיה כ:ו) "ואתה פשחור וכל יושבי ביתך תלכו בשבי ושם תמות ושמה תקבר", הוי יש בידו שתי מיתות. לפיכך יעקב אומר ליוסף "אל נא תקברני במצרים."
א"ר סימון א"כ הפסידו הצדיקים שהם קבורים בחוצה לארץ! אלא מה הקב"ה עושה? עושה להן מחילות בארץ, ועושה אותן כמערות הללו, והן מתגלגלין ובאים עד שהם מגיעין לארץ ישראל, והקדוש ברוך הוא נותן בהם רוח של חיים והן עומדין. מנין? שכן כתיב (יחזקאל לז:יב) "הנה אני פותח את קברותיכם והעליתי אתכם מקברותיכם עמי והבאתי אתכם אל אדמת ישראל", ואחר כך ונתתי רוחי בכם וחייתם." אמר ריש לקיש מקרא מלא הוא, שכיון שהן מגיעין לארץ ישראל הקב"ה נותן בהם נשמה שנאמר (ישעיה מב:ה) "נותן נשמה לעם עליה."
מעשה ברבי ורבי אליעזר שהיו מהלכין בפילי שחוץ לטבריא. ראו ארון של מת שבא מחוצה לארץ להקבר בארץ ישראל. אמר רבי לר' אליעזר מה הועיל זה שיצתה נשמתו בחוץ לארץ ובא להקבר בארץ ישראל? אני קורא עליו (ירמיה ב:ז) "ונחלתי שמתם לתועבה", "בחייכם, "ותבאו ותטמאו את ארצי", במיתתכם. א"ל כיון שהוא נקבר בארץ ישראל, הקדוש ברוך הוא מכפר לו, דכתיב (דברים לב:מג) "וכפר אדמתו עמו.

Why did all our forefathers ask for and treasure being buried in Eretz Yisrael? Rabbi Elazar said, There is a secret here. Rabbi Yehoshua ben Levi said, What secret is there here? (Tehillim 117:9) "I will go before Hashem in the lands of the living."

Our rabbis said two things in the name of Rabbi Chelbo. Why did our forefathers treasure being buried in Eretz Yisrael? Because the dead of Eretz Yisrael will be the first to be brought back to life in the days of Moshiach, and they will enjoy the days of Moshiach. Rabbi Chanina said, One who dies in Chutz La'aretz and is buried there has two deaths in his hand, for it is written, (Yirmiya 20:6) "And you, Pashchor, and all who dwell in your house will go in captivity, and there you will die, and there you will be buried." Thus he has in his hands two deaths. Therefore Yaacov said to Yosef, "Please do not bury me in Egypt."

Rabbi Simon said, If so, the righteous who are buried in Chutz La'aretz have lost out! Rather, what will Hakadosh Baruch Hu do? He will make tunnels for them in the land, and make them like passageways, and they will keep rolling until they reach Eretz Yisrael. Then Hakadosh Baruch Hu will give in them a spirit of life, and they will arise. How do we know? For it is written, (Yechezkel 37:12) "Behold, I will open your graves and bring you up from your graves, My people, and I will bring you to the earth of Israel" and afterwards "and I will give My spirit in you and you will live."

Reish Lakish said, It is an explicit verse, that once they reach Eretz Yisrael, Hakadosh Baruch Hu will place a soul in them, as it says, (Yeshaya 42:5) "Who places a soul for the people upon it."

It happened that Rebbe and Rabbi Eliezer were walking by the gates outside Teverya. They saw the coffin of a dead person who had come from Chutz La'aretz to be buried in Eretz Yisrael. Rebbe said to Rabbi Eliezer, "What good is it that this person whose soul left him in Chutz La'aretz has come to be buried in Eretz Yisrael? I read regarding him, 'And My inheritance they treated as an abomination' — during your lifetime — 'and you came and defiled My land' (Yirmiya 2:7) — after your death."

He said back to him, "Once he is buried in Eretz Yisrael, Hakadosh Baruch Hu atones for him, as it is written, (Devarim 32:43) 'And His land atones for His people.'"

Once again, we see the great importance Chazal placed on

coming to Eretz Yisrael — alive! We also see the disdain Rebbe had for those who failed to come in their lifetimes, despite the "consolation prize" for those who are at least buried in Eretz Yisrael, and the magnanimous sentiments for righteous people who weren't fortunate enough to merit either.

Devarim Rabba 2:8 states:

אמר רבי לוי אמר לפניו, רבש"ע! עצמותיו של יוסף נכנסו לארץ ואני איני נכנס לארץ? אמר לו הקב"ה, מי שהודה בארצו נקבר בארצו, ומי שלא הודה בארצו אינו נקבר בארצו. יוסף הודה בארצו מנין? גבירתו אומרת (בראשית לט:יד) "ראו הביא לנו איש עברי וגו'" ולא כפר אלא (שם מ:טו) "גנב גנבתי מארץ העברים", נקבר בארצו מנין? שנאמר (יהושע כד:לב) "ואת עצמות יוסף אשר העלו מארץ מצרים קברו בשכם", את שלא הודית בארצך אין אתה נקבר בארצך. כיצד? בנות יתרו אומרות (שמות ב:יט) "איש מצרי הצילנו מיד הרועים", והוא שומע ושותק, לפיכך לא נקבר בארצו.

Rabbi Levi said, He [Moshe] said before Him, "Master of the universe! The bones of Yosef get to enter the land, and I don't get to enter the land?" Hakadosh Baruch Hu said to him, "He who acknowledged his association with the land is buried in his land, and he who did not acknowledge his association with his land is not buried in his land."

From where do we know Yosef acknowledged his association with his land? His mistress said (Bereishis 39:14) "See! A Hebrew was brought to us," and he did not deny it, but said, (Bereishis 40:15) "For I was surely kidnapped from the land of the Hebrews." How do we know he is buried in his land? As it says, (Yehoshua 24:32) "And the bones of Yosef that they brought up from the land of Egypt they buried in Shechem."

[Said Hashem,] "You, who did not acknowledge your association with your land, will not be buried in the land." How is this? The daughters of Yisro said (Shemos 2:19), "An Egyptian man rescued us from the shepherds," and he heard this and was quiet. Therefore, he is not buried in his land.

The Maharzu notes:

ואע"פ שמשה לא היה מעולם בארץ העברים כיוסף, שהרי משה נולד במצרים, וי"ל שגם במצרים נקראו ישראל עברים, כמ"ש "והנה שני אנשים עברים נצים", "איש מצרי מכה איש עברי" ומשה אמר "אלהי

"העברים".

Even though Moshe was never in the land of the Hebrews as Yosef was, for Moshe was born in Egypt [and thus it seems unfair to compare the two], we can say that the Jewish people were also called Hebrews in Egypt, as it is written "And behold two Hebrews were fighting," and "An Egyptian man was striking a Hebrew man," and Moshe said, "The God of the Hebrews."

It is clear from these sources that the Jewish people are always supposed to identify with the Land of Israel and consider it their homeland. This was true even before the Torah was given, and certainly remains true today!

It is frightening to consider the fact that so many *galus* Jews not only fail to correct people who misidentify them, but explicitly disassociate themselves from the Land of Israel, wishing to be identified only as members of other nations and citizens of lands not their own. Hopefully these Torah sources will open their eyes and inspire them to do *teshuva* before it is too late.

A mitzvah *even in our times*

Rabbi Eliezer ben Moshe Ascari, who lived in Tzfat long before Moshiach came, and was buried there after his passing in 1600, stated in no uncertain terms that living in Eretz Yisrael is a *mitzvah* from the Torah, even in our times.

Copied below are two citations from his classic work, which, ironically, is called Sefer Chareidim. The first concludes his enumeration and discussion of the 613 commandments, and the second is a chapter dedicated entirely to the *mitzvah* of living in Eretz Yisrael. Due to the length of the sources, translation and commentary will follow each paragraph.

מצות עשה מן התורה לדור בארץ ישראל, שנאמר (דברים כו:א) "וירשתה וישבת בה.". ואמרו רז"ל בספרי (ראה כח) שמצוה זו שקולה כנגד כל המצות התורה. ואמרו (כתובות קי:) כל היוצא מארץ ישראל כו' יהיה בעיניך כעובד אלילים, שנאמר (ש"א כו:יט) "כי גרשוני היום מהסתפח בנחלת ה' לאמר לך עבוד אלהים אחרים." ואיתא במסכת בתרא (צא.) אמר רשב"י דאלימלך ומחלון וכליון נענשו מפני שיצאו מארץ ישראל למואב, שנאמר (רות א:יט) "ותהום כל העיר עליהם ותאמרנה הזאת נעמי." אמר רבי יצחק, אמרו חזיתם נעמי שיצאת מארץ ישראל למואב מה עלתה לה. אמר ר' יהושע בן קרחה, ח"ו שאפילו מצאו סובין לא יצאו, ומפני מה נענשו, מפני שהיה להם לבקש רחמים על בני דורם ולא בקשו. עד כאן ממנין תרי"ג לרמב"ן ולרשב"ץ.

It is a positive commandment from the Torah to reside in Eretz Yisrael, as it says (Devarim 26:1) "And you shall inherit it and settle in it." And our Rabbis of blessed memory said in Sifrei (Re'ei 28) that this mitzvah is of equivalent weight to all the mitzvos of the Torah. And they said (Kesbuos 110b) "All who go out from the Land of Israel...should be in your eyes like idolaters, as it says (Shmuel I 26:19) 'For they have driven me out today from being connected with the inheritance of Hashem, saying go serve other gods.'"

And it is brought in Bava Basra (91a): Rabbi Shimon bar Yochai said that Elimelech, Machlon, and Chilyon were punished because they left Eretz Yisrael for Moav, as it says (Ruth 1:19): "And all the city was in an uproar over them, and they said, 'Is this Naomi?'" Rabbi Yitzchak said, They said, "Have you seen Naomi, who left Eretz Yisrael for Moav, what happened to her?"

Rabbi Yehoshua ben Korcha said, God forbid! Even if they found bran they wouldn't have left.

Why were they punished? Because they should have pleaded for mercy for the people of their generation, and they did not.

This concludes the enumeration of the 613 commandments according to the Ramban and the Rashbetz.

According to several sages who enumerated the 613 Torah commandments, living in Eretz Yisrael is one of them — a commandment that is incumbent in principle on every Jew, irrespective of whether or not Moshiach has come or whether or not we were exiled from the land.

It cannot be argued that there is a fundamental disagreement over whether living in Eretz Yisrael is a timeless Torah commandment, or purely optional, or even prohibited, until Moshiach comes. There is also no indication of this in all the numerous sources from Chazal on the subject of living in Eretz Yisrael, including the Midrash cited on Ruth.

The Sefer Chareidim continues in an entire chapter dedicated to this *mitzvah*:

וצריך כל איש ישראל לחבב את ארץ ישראל ולבא אליה מאפסי ארץ בתשוקה גדולה כבן אל חיק אמו, כי תחילת עווננו שקבע לנו בכיה לדורות יען מאסנו בה, שנאמר (תהלים קו:כד) "וימאסו בארץ חמדה." ובפדיון נפשנו מהרה יהיה כתיב (שם קב:טו,יד) "כי רצו עבדיך את אבניה ואת עפרה יחוננו וגו'." אתה תקום תרחם ציון. ולפיכך היו האמוראים מנשקים עפרותה ואבניה בבואם אליה.

ומה טוב ומה נעים לשיר שיר ידידות אשר יסד ר' יהודה הלוי עליה באהבה רבה, תחילת השירה ארץ הקדושה יקרה חמודה וכו', כן אנו

משוררים על ציון ר' יהודה בר אלעי כל ערב ראש חודש בשמחה רבה, ומתחננים לאל אל יגרשנו מעליה.

גם הקרובים והרחוקים אשר חוצה לה ראוי להם שיהיו נכספים ותאבים אליה, כי כשם שבחר בהם, כך בחר בארץ ישראל ויחד אותה להם. ואין נקראים גוי אחד אלא עמה, שכך פירש רשב"י על מקרא שכתוב (דה"א יז:כא) "ומי כעמך ישראל גוי אחד בארץ."

Every Jewish person needs to treasure the Land of Israel and come to it from the ends of the earth with great yearning, like a child to the bosom of his mother, for the first of our sins that established for us crying for generations was because we rejected it, as it says (Tehillim 106:24) "And they rejected the precious land." And regarding the redemption of our souls, let it be quickly, it is written (Tehillim 102:15,14) "For Your servants cherish its stones and desire its dust...You will rise and have mercy on Zion." Therefore the Amoraim would kiss its dust and stones when they came to it.

And how good and pleasant it is to sing the song of friendship that Rabbi Yehuda HaLevi composed about it with great love. The beginning of the song is "The holy land, precious and dear, etc." So we sing over the gravestone of Rabbi Yehuda bar Ila'i every Rosh Chodesh eve with great joy, and we beseech God not to expel us from upon it.

Also those who are outside it from near and far should yearn for and desire it, for just as He chose them, so He chose the Land of Israel and designated it for them. And we are not called one nation except with it, for this is how Rabbi Shimon bar Yochai explained the verse in which it is written (Divrei Hayamim I 17:21) "And who is like your people, Israel, one nation in the land."

ומצינו במדרש שהקב"ה אמר לאברהם אבינו פעם ראשונה, שילך לארץ ישראל ויראנה ויחזור. ואחר שחזר, לא נתן לו רשות לחזור לארץ ישראל עד חמש שנים, ואותן חמש שנים היה משתוקק לחזור ללכת, והוא אמר זה הפסוק (תהלים נה:ז) "מי יתן לי אבר כיונה אעופה ואשכונה הנה ארחיק נדוד אלין במדבר סלה." מוטב ללין במדבריות של ארץ ישראל, ולא ללין בסלטריות של חוצה לארץ, והיה תאב. ומשהורשה כתיב (בראשית יב:ד) "וילך אברם כאשר דבר אליו ה'."

וקודם בואו אל הארץ לא היה משתוקק, אבל אחר שבא שמה פעם ראשונה וראה במראה הנבואה יקר תפארת קדושת הארץ, אז נכסף נכסוף. וממנו נלמוד לדורות אנחנו יוצאי חלציו להיות נכספים כמוהו, אע"פ שיושביה בצער, על מנת כך נהיה שמחים ביסורין.

And we find in the Midrash that Hakadosh Baruch Hu said to our father Avraham the first time that he should go to Eretz Yisrael, see it, and return. And after he returned, He did not give him permission to return to Eretz Yisrael for five years, and for those five years he was yearning to return and go, and he said this verse (Tehillim 55:7) "If only he would give me wings like a dove, I would fly and dwell. I would go off to the distance and dwell in the desert," [as if to say] it is better to stay in the deserts of Eretz Yisrael rather than the fine lodgings of Chutz La'aretz, and he was yearning. And when he was permitted it is written (Bereishis 12:4) "And Avram went as Hashem spoke to him."

Before he came to the land he was not craving it, but after he came there one time and saw in a prophetic vision the precious glory of the holiness of the land, then he greatly desired it. And from this we learn for the generations, we, his descendants, to desire it just as he did, even though those who live there are in a state of pain — for this sake we are happy to suffer.

וזהו טעם סמיכות פרשת עמלק וביאת ארץ ישראל בפרשת כי תבא (דברים כה:יז) כמו שאמרו רז"ל (ברכות ה.) ג' מתנות נתן הקב"ה לישראל ולא נתנם אלא ע"י יסורין, ואלו הן תורה וארץ ישראל ועולם הבא. וכי היכי דבביאה ראשונה בא עמלק, הכי נמי בכיבוש גליות כשרוצים לבא לארץ ישראל עמלק מזדמן להם בדרך, וכאשר עינינו רואות היום תמיד, ירא ה' וישפוט.

This is the reason that the chapter of Amalek is juxtaposed with coming to Eretz Yisrael in Parashas Ki Savo (Devarim 25:17) as our Rabbis of blessed memory said (Brachos 5a) "Hashem gave three gifts to Israel, and He only gave them through affliction, and these are them: Torah, Eretz Yisrael, and the world to come." Just as when we first were coming to the land Amalek came, so too when the exiled ones conquer it, when they want to come to Eretz Yisrael, Amalek is ready for them on the way, as we see with our own eyes constantly. Hashem should see and judge.

והתחיל בתיבת "והיה" (דברים כה:יט) הוא אחד משנים עשר צרופים של השם הקדוש, רמז כי הדר בארץ ישראל דבק בה' הפך הדר בחוץ לארץ היינו הישראלי שדומה למי שאין לו אלוה. ונקט צירוף זה, רמז למה שאמרו רז"ל (בר"ר מב:ג) כל מקום שנאמר והיה לשון שמחה הוא, וכתב הרמב"ן במנין תרי"ג, מצות ישיבת ארץ ישראל כל עת ורגע

שהאדם בארץ ישראל הוא מקיים המצוה הזו.
וידוע שעיקר שכר המצוה על השמחה גדולה כדכתיב (דברים כח:מז) "תחת אשר לא עבדת את ה' אלהיך בשמחה", א"כ צריך היושב בארץ ישראל להיות שמח תדיר במצוותו התדירה באהבת אותה. וגם צריך להיות ירא וחרד, כדכתב רשב"י (עי' תקו"ז תקון י כה:ב) כל פקודא דלאו איהו ברחימו ודחילו לאו פקודא היא, לכך אמרו באבות דר' נתן (צ"ל מס' דרך ארץ ב) הוי שש וחרד על המצות. והנה תיבת והיה אצל מצות ישיבת ארץ ישראל, רמז לשמחת המצוה. וסמיכת הפרשה לעמלק, רמז לחרדה במצות מהרצועה התלויה באויר.

And it began with the word "Vehaya" (Devarim 25:19) which is one of the twelve combinations of the letters of the Holy Name, which hints that one who dwells in Eretz Yisrael is attached to Hashem, the opposite of one who dwells in Chutz La'aretz — that is the Israelite — is similar to one who has no God.

It specifically used this combination as a hint to what our rabbis of blessed memory said (Bereishis Rabba 42:3) "Wherever it says 'Vehaya' indicates joy." And the Ramban writes in his enumeration of the 613 commandments, "Regarding the mitzvah of settling Eretz Yisrael, all the time and every moment that a person spends in Eretz Yisrael he fulfills this mitzvah."

And it is known that the main reward for a mitzvah is for the great happiness [with which one performs it], as it is written (Devarim 28:47) "[This happened] because you did not serve God...with happiness." That being the case, one who resides in Eretz Yisrael must always be happy with his constant mitzvah, with his great love for it.

He also needs to be afraid and trembling, as Rabbi Shimon bar Yochai writes (see Tikkunei Hazohar, Tikkun 10 25:2) "Any mitzvah that is not done with love and fear is not a mitzvah." Therefore they said in Avos D'Rabbi Nathan (it should say Tractate Derech Eretz 2) "Be joyous and trembling over the mitzvos."

Behold the word "Vehaya" appears by the mitzvah of settling Eretz Yisrael, hinting to the joy of the mitzvah, and the juxtaposition to the chapter of Amalek is a hint to trembling for the mitzvos from the strap [of punishment] that is hanging in the air.

ויסורין של ארץ ישראל, הן מן הישמעאלים, הן מן החלאים, מזבח כפרה הם, כדבר שנאמר (ישעיה לג:כד) "ובל יאמר שכן חליתי העם היושב בה נשוא עון." וזה רמז ג"כ בפסוק זה (דברים כו:א) בסופי תיבות והיה כי

תבוא אל הארץ אשר ה' אלהיך נותן לך נחלה, נכ"ה והוא מלשון (חולין פ"י מ"ג) מנכה לו מן הדמים, וכדפירש רש"י בפסוק (במדבר כב:ו) "אולי אוכל נכה בו", ופירוש העניין שעל ידי הצרות שבארץ ישראל מתנכים ומתמעטים העוונות, והעם היושב בה נשוא עון. וכתיב (דברים לב:מג) "וכפר אדמתו עמו." ודוקא בעוונות קלים, ששבים ומתחרטים עליהם ויסורין אלו ממרקין, ובעת מותו של אדם הולך נכוחו לגן עדן.

And the afflictions of Eretz Yisrael, whether from the Ishmaelites or from illnesses, are an altar of atonement, like that which it says (Yeshaya 33:24) "And no one who lives there shall say 'I have become ill', for the people who dwell there have their sins lifted." And it is written (Devarim 32:43) "And the land is an atonement for His people." This refers specifically to light sins, for which they repent and regret, and these afflictions cleanse them, and when a person dies he goes straight to Gan Eden.

אבל הבאים לארץ ישראל ואין שמים על לבביהם בהיכל המלך, ומורדים ופושעים ומרבים במשתאות של סעודות מרעות ומרזחים, עליהם הכתוב אומר (ירמיה ב:ז) "ותבאו ותטמאו את ארצי ונחלתי שמתם לתועבה", וכתיב (ישעיה א:יב) "כי תבואו לראות פני מי בקש זאת מידכם רמוס חצרי", ולא יעלה על לבם שאחרי מותם ישארו בארץ ישראל, אלא במותם יגרשום חוצה ככלבים. וזה לשון פרקי דרבי אליעזר (לג) "וכל הרשעים המתים בארץ ישראל נפשותם נשלכות [בקלע] חוצה לארץ שנאמר (ש"א כה:כט) "ואת נפש אויביך יקלענה בתוך כף הקלע", ולעתיד לבא הקב"ה אוחז בכנפות הארץ ומנער אותה מכל טומאה ומשליכן לחוץ (לארץ) שנאמר (איוב לח:יג) "לאחוז בכנפות הארץ וינערו רשעים ממנה."

But those who come to Eretz Yisrael and don't have regard that they are in the King's court, and they rebel and sin and have an abundance of feasts and parties — about them the scripture says (Yirmiya 2:7) "And they came and defiled My land, and they made My inheritance into an abomination," and it is written (Yeshaya 1:12) "When you come to see My face, who asked you to trample My courtyards?"

And you shouldn't entertain the idea that after their death they will remain in Eretz Yisrael, but after their death they will be driven out like dogs. And this is the language in Pirkei D'Rabbi Eliezer (33) "And all the wicked who die in Eretz Yisrael, their souls are cast out of the land with a slingshot, as it says (Shmuel I 25:29) 'And the soul of your *enemies should be thrown about in a slingshot,' and in the coming future Hakadosh Baruch Hu will take hold of the ends of the land and shake out from it all of the impurity and cast it out of the land, as it says (Iyov 38:13) "To take hold of the ends of the land and shake out the wicked from it."*

וכתב הרמב"ן בפרשת אחרי מות, שהזכיר הכתוב בעריות (ויקרא יח:כה) "ותטמא הארץ ואפקוד עונה", אע"פ שהעריות חובת הגוף ואינן תלויות בארץ, מכל מקום עיקר כל המצות ליושבים בארץ ה'. וכן שנו בספרא (קדושים יב:יד) "ולא תקיא הארץ אתכם" (ויקרא יח:כח) ארץ ישראל אינה כשאר ארצות, אינה מקיימת עוברי עבירה. והנה הכותיים לא היו נענשים בארצם, ובבואם בארץ ה' ועשו שם כמעשיהם הראשונים, שלח בהם האריות הממיתים אותם. לכן כל איש יחרד בבואו אל ארץ ישראל להיות ירא שמים כפלי כפלים ממה שהיה בחוץ לארץ, וידע כי בבית המלך הוא יושב.

And the Ramban writes in Parashas Acharei Mos, where the scripture mentioned immorality (Vayikra 18:25) "And the land was defiled and I visited its sin [upon it]," that even though [the commandments regarding] immorality are duties of the body and not dependent on the land, nevertheless all the mitzvos are primarily for those who dwell in the land of Hashem. And so it was taught in the Sifra (Kedoshim 12:14) "'And the land should not vomit you out' (Yayikra 18:28): Eretz Yisrael is not like other lands, for it does not uphold sinners."

Behold, the Cuthites were not punished [for idolatry] in their land, and when they came to the land of Hashem and did there like their original deeds, He sent lions against them that killed them. Therefore, every man should tremble when he comes to Eretz Yisrael, to have fear of Heaven many times over what he had in Chutz La'aretz, and he should know that he is living in the house of the King.

The words of the Sefer Chareidim are so clear and direct that anything more than a summation of his main points with brief additional comments would be superfluous:

1) There is no restriction on living in Eretz Yisrael until Moshiach comes — quite the contrary, it is a timeless *mitzvah*.

2) We should cherish the opportunity to live in Eretz Yisrael, and do so with great happiness, despite the inconveniences and even suffering this might entail.

3) It is better to live in the worst parts of Eretz Yisrael than the best places outside the land.

4) We were exiled from Eretz Yisrael in the first place largely because we did not appreciate it.

Let us not continue to make the same mistake, lest this prevent us from regaining what we lost, God forbid.

5) Those who do not yet dwell in Eretz Yisrael should truly be pained by this and yearn to live in Eretz Yisrael. For this to be genuine, this must be accompanied by concrete actions to fulfill this yearning, barring truly extenuating circumstances.

6) The Land of Israel is a vital and inseparable part of our identity as a nation. Naturally, this does not mean merely paying homage to the land, but living there or striving to live there.

7) We should expect Amalek to seek to prevent us from returning to Eretz Yisrael and making life difficult for those who return. This is not to be taken as a sign that Hashem doesn't want us to return to Eretz Yisrael, but that we need to earn it. We need to revere what it means to live in Eretz Yisrael.

8) At the same time, we should not shirk the *mitzvah* to live in Eretz Yisrael and the responsibilities that come with that. We should do our best to increase our fear of Heaven and rise to the occasion. If we are sincerely trying, merely living in the land will atone for many of our sins.

A wise move

The Sefer Habris writes as follows in chapter 2 of essay 7, Da'as Ruach:

יש אויר מחכים, והוא בארץ ישראל, כמו שאמרו חז"ל (בבא בתרא דף קנח) אוירא דארץ ישראל מחכים, ועל ישרי לב אשר היכולת בידם ויברך אותם אלקים בעושר תמהני שאינם בוחרים לדור בארץ אשר ה' דורש אותה תמיד מדור בארץ לא להם, ואלו היה נמצא ארץ אשר אוירה מעשיר בלי ספק שהיו נוסעים והולכים לשבת בארץ ההיא.
וכמה ראוי לכל איש ישראל אשר היכולת בידו לרוץ אורח לדור לארץ מולדתנו אחוזת אבותינו, כאשר ירוצו התינוקות אל חיק אמותם במרוצה גדולה ושמחה רבה, כי אנו לא נקראים עם אחד כי עם [אולי צ"ל אם] בצירוף הארץ הקדושה ההיא, בסוד ועשיתי אותם לגוי אחד בארץ בהרי ישראל (יחזקאל לז), ומה רב טוב הצפון לקדושים אשר בארץ המה, וכבר האריך בענין זה בטוב טעם ודעת הגאון יעב"ץ ז"ל בהקדמת סדר תפלה שלו.

There is air that brings wisdom, and that is in Eretz Yisrael, as Chazal said (Bava Basra 158b) "The air of Eretz Yisrael brings wisdom," and those who are straight of heart with the ability in their hands, and Hashem blessed them with wealth — I wonder why they don't choose to dwell in the land that Hashem seeks out constantly, rather than dwelling in a land that is not theirs. And were there to be found a land whose air brings wealth, without a doubt they would travel and go to live in that land.

How appropriate it is for every Jewish man with the ability in his hand to run on the way to dwell in our homeland, the possession of our fathers, just as children run to the bosom of their mothers with great rushing and joy, for we are only called one people in conjunction with this holy land, as is the secret [meaning of] "And I made them one nation in the land, in the mountains of Israel" (Yechezkel 37:22). How great is the goodness that is hidden away for the holy people in that land, and the Ya'avetz, of blessed memory, already discussed this matter at length with good reasoning and intelligence in the introduction to his prayer book.

The Sefer Habris — who lived in the 1700s in Vilna and other parts of Europe – takes it for granted that anyone with his head in the right place and the means to do so would run to live in Eretz Yisrael.

There can be no doubt that the challenges and sacrifices involved with moving to Eretz Yisrael in his time, even for people of means, were exponentially greater than those that pass for insurmountable hurdles in our time, even for people of modest means. If the Sefer Habris was astonished that wealthy Torah-observant Jews didn't run to Eretz Yisrael back then, where they were sure to face hardship and deprivation, what would he say about the pampered, excuse-laden *galus* Jews of today who forsake their homeland without a second thought?

How can strictly religious Jews forsake living in Eretz Yisrael?

Here is a short excerpt from the lengthy introduction of the Ya'avetz (Rav Yaacov Emden) to his siddur:

קול קורא פנו דרך העם הרימו מכשול, לזרז לבוא אליה בלי רישול. ובאמת היא תמיהא קיימת על ישראל קדושים בכל מקום הם החמירו על עצמן בכמה דקדוקי מצות שהחזיקו בהם מדקדקים בהם ביותר מפזרים ממון רב וטורחים מאד לקיימן בשלמות האפשרי. ומדוע מזלזלין ומתעצלין במצוה החביבה הזאת, יתד שכל התורה תלויה בו?

A call goes out, clear the way for the people, remove the obstacles, hasten to come to her [Eretz Yisrael and Jerusalem] without laxity. And it is truly an ongoing astonishment that holy Jews everywhere are stringent with themselves on many details of mitzvos to which they hold fast; they are exceedingly particular with them, spending a great deal of money and troubling themselves very much to fulfill them in the most complete way possible — so why are they scornful and lazy with this precious mitzvah, a peg on which the entire Torah hangs?

The following is a summary of many related points from pages 69-74 in the introduction to Rav Emden's *siddur*, which can be viewed at https://www.hebrewbooks.org/pdfpager.aspx?req=22431&st=&pgnum=69.

Rav Emden goes on to reassure those who are concerned about the difficult journey to Eretz Yisrael (compare to today) that the reward is commensurate with the trouble. Furthermore, he writes, when one considers the precarious state of the Jews in *galus*, it will be easy for him to look towards Hashem and seek out his inheritance.

He especially reassures wealthy people that there are plenty of business opportunities in Eretz Yisrael, while discouraging them from being overly preoccupied with worldly matters and defiling the land. Those who have wealth, property, and all they desire, but fail to purchase a home in "this good land" and experience true joy from all their toil, suffer from foolishness and a terrible illness.

Rav Emden also writes at length about Torah scholars in *galus* who have no interest in returning to Eretz Yisrael. He declares that their Torah learning is not for the sake of Heaven, because the Torah can best be learned only in Eretz Yisrael, and much of the Torah can only be fulfilled in Eretz Yisrael. Since they forsake the land, they forget much of their learning, and Torah is belittled in the eyes of the people. Eretz Yisrael itself complains about its shame and metaphorically seeks its blood from their hands, for it is on their account that all the good and fatness of the land has been lost.

Rav Emden laments that he was unable to move to Eretz Yisrael sooner due to circumstances beyond his control (specifically wars that made the journey impossible, and lack of means). He writes that, despite being blessed with a good living situation in *galus*, he constantly had his focus on moving to Eretz Yisrael, and intended to do so at the earliest opportunity.

He then instructs his children to move to Eretz Yisrael after getting married at 18, saving up money for the journey, and having a means of livelihood, however scant. At that point they should not delay, but settle permanently in Eretz Yisrael without fear of the nations or lack of sustenance.

Finally, Rav Emden writes that those who make a firm decision to return to Eretz Yisrael when they are able, but are forced to remain in *galus*, will benefit from their good intentions. Their prayers will be accepted as if they are standing in Eretz Yisrael, opposite the gates of Heaven, and this will help them to fulfill their intentions.

If Rav Emden was so dismayed by the intransigence of the *galus* Jews in his time, what would he say about the *galus* Jews today?

A mitzvah *to help others move to Eretz Yisrael*

The Peleh Yoetz, published in 1824 by Rabbi Eliezer Papo, repeatedly emphasizes the great merit and importance of living in Eretz Yisrael — before Moshiach comes. A few examples:

In his essay on הרשאה (power of attorney) he generally discourages people from getting involved in other people's financial affairs and litigations. But then he writes:

אמנם יש אפנים שאי אפשר לומר ונקה מלהיות מרשה, כגון אם אביו ואחיו הולכים לארץ ישראל והניחו מעותם ביד אחרים שצריך לפקח על עסקיהם ועל נכסיהם, כי מי יחוס עליהם יותר ממנו? ואפלו אם איש זר הולך לארץ ישראל ואין לו קרובים לסמך עליהם ואינו מוצא איש הגון שיפקח על עסקיו, במקום שאין אנשים חיובא רמיא לעשות חסד גדול כזה לזכות נפש מישראל שילך לארץ הקדושה.

> However, there are instances when it is impossible to absolve oneself from being a legal representative, for example, if his father or brother are going to Eretz Yisrael and they left their money in the hands of others, in which case he has to watch over their affairs and their property, for who will take greater concern for them than him?
>
> And even if a stranger is going to Eretz Yisrael and he has no relatives to rely upon, and he cannot find an appropriate person to watch over his affairs, in a place where there is no man, there is an obligation to do great kindness like this, to give a Jewish soul the merit of going to the Holy Land.

The Peleh Yoetz expresses no reservations about aiding people in violating an oath. In his essay on דירה (residence) he writes as follows:

וגם בערים יבחר אדם באיזה עיר ידור כאשר כתבתי במקום אחר, ובפרט לדור בארץ ישראל, שהרי אמרו (כתובות קי:) הדר בארץ ישראל דומה כמי שיש לו אלוה וכו'. וידוע שירושלים מקדשת מכל ארץ ישראל, ולכן מי שחשקה נפשו וטורח לשכון כבוד בארצנו יבחר לו הטוב, טוב לקבע דירתו בירושלים עיר הקדש, תבנה ותכונן במהרה בימינו, אם לא שחושב שבעיר אחרת יהיה לו יותר ישוב לעבודת השם יתברך, שאז אפלו ישיבת חוצה לארץ טובה משיבת ארץ ישראל...ועל כל פנים לעת זקנתו עת לחננה על הנשמה להשיב הפקדון אל האלקים, אשר בכחו לעשות יעשה לעלות אל מקום המזבח שם תהא מיתתו שם תהא קבורתו והיתה כבוד מנוחתו. על זאת יתפלל כל ימי היותו, כמאמר דוד המלך עליו השלום (תהלים כז:ד) "אחת שאלתי מאת ה' וכו' לחזות בנעם ה' ולבקר בהיכלו" אולי ישמע ה' קולו.

    And one should also choose which city to reside in, as I wrote elsewhere, and specifically to dwell in Eretz Yisrael, for they said (Kesubos 110b) "One who dwells in Eretz Yisrael is like one who has a God..." And it is known that Jerusalem is holier than all of Eretz Yisrael; therefore one whose soul yearns and is striving to live in glory in our land should choose the best — best to establish his dwelling in Jerusalem, the holy city, may it be built and established quickly in our days, unless he thinks he will have a better opportunity to serve Hashem in a different city, in which case even living in Chutz La'aretz is better than living in Eretz Yisrael...

    ...In any case, when he gets old, when it is time to be gracious to his soul to return the deposit to God, he should do what is in his power to go up to the place of the altar. There he should die, and there he should be buried, and his resting will be with honor. He should pray for this all his days, as King David of blessed memory said (Tehillim 27:4) "I asked for one thing from Hashem...to gaze at the pleasantness of Hashem and to visit His sanctuary." Maybe Hashem will hear his voice.

    Misguided Jews who tragically want to remain in exile will eagerly pounce on the caveat of the Peleh Yoetz, that one who believes he can serve Hashem better outside of Eretz Yisrael should do so, and sanctimoniously misappropriate this exemption for themselves. Clearly that is not the intention of the Peleh Yoetz. On the contrary, he gives a begrudging nod to the reality of individual circumstances that sometimes trump even the overarching priority of living in Eretz Yisrael. Even those who truly must remain in *galus* for reasons of serving Hashem better should do so mournfully and pine for the day when they can live in Eretz Yisrael.

Older people, whose sphere of activity in serving Hashem has become more narrow anyway, should especially make an effort to live out their final days in Eretz Yisrael, and achieve the great merit of living there, passing on there, and being buried there, as we saw earlier.

Indeed, in his essay on כבוד אב ואם he writes:

ובכלל כבוד אב ואם להשתדל בכל עז לזכות נפשם לשלחם לארץ ישראל, ואפלו אם קשה עליו פרדתם והוצאתם, הכל כאין נגד הנחת רוח שעושה להם בזכותו את נפשם, ובזה יתרצה על אשר חטא כנגדם.

The mitzvah to honor one's father and mother includes striving with all one's might to bring merit to their souls to send them to Eretz Yisrael. Even if their separation and sending them out is hard for him, it is all nothing compared to the soothing of the spirit he does for them when he brings merit to their souls, and with this he will find appeasement over that which he sinned against them.

In his essay on כללות he cites the Sefer Chareidim that we saw earlier:

מצוה רבה לחבב את ארץ ישראל ולבוא אליה מאפסי הארץ בתשוקה גדולה כבן אל חיק אמו.

It is a great mitzvah to cherish Eretz Yisrael and to come to it from the ends of the earth with great yearning, like a child to his mother's bosom.

Finally, in his essay on צדקה he writes:

ובכלל אמרם "חייך קודמין" הוא שימכר קרקעות ומטלטלין ויכלכל את שיבתו, ויזכה נפשו לשכן כבוד בארץ הקדש, ויטל חלק בראש לשלח לעולם הבא מעדנים לנפשו, ואל יחוש כל כך על בניו להניח להם כל חילו, כי אדם קרוב אצל עצמו וחייו קודמים.

Included in what they said "your life comes first" is that he should sell his land and assets in order to sustain himself in his old age, and bring merit to his soul with the honor of dwelling in the holy land, and he should take the first portion to send delights for his soul in the world to come, and not be so concerned for his children to leave them all his wealth, for a person's closest relation is himself, and his life comes first.

Worth more than all the money in the world

The Sifrei on Devarim 11:17 is a stinging rebuke for the many Jews who choose to remain in *galus* for materialistic reasons:

"וחרה אף ה'", אחר כל היסורים שאני מביא עליכם אני מגלה אתכם. קשה גלות ששקולה כנגד הכל, שנאמר (דברים כט:כז) "ויתשם ה' מעל אדמתם באף ובחימה ובקצף גדול וישליכם אל ארץ אחרת כיום הזה", ואומר (ירמיה טו:ב) "והיה כי יאמרו אליך אנה נצא ואמרת אליהם כה אמר ה' אשר למות למות ואשר לחרב לחרב ואשר לרעב לרעב ואשר לשבי לשבי", ואומר (עמוס ז:יז) "כה אמר ה' אשתך בעיר תזנה ובניך ובנותיך בחרב יפולו ואדמתך בחבל תחולק ואתה על אדמה טמאה תמות וישראל גלה יגלה מעל אדמתו", ואומר (ירמיה כב:י) "אל תבכו למת ואל תנודו לו בכו בכו להולך כי לא ישוב עוד וראה את ארץ מולדתו."
"אל תבכו למת", זה יהויקים מלך יהודה. מה נאמר בו? (שם כב:יט) "קבורת חמור יקבר וגו'" "בכו בכו להולך", זה יהויכין מלך יהודה. מה נאמר בו? (שם נב:לג-לד) "ושנה את בגדי כלאו וארוחתו וגו'." נמצינו למידים שנבלת יהויקים מלך יהודה, שהיתה מושלכת לחורב ביום ולקרח בלילה חביבה מחייו של יהויכין מלך יהודה, שהיה כסאו מעל כסא המלכים ואוכל ושותה בטרקליני מלכים.

"And the wrath of Hashem will be kindled": After all the afflictions I bring upon you I will exile you. Exile is harsh, for it weighs as much as everything else, as it says (Devarim 29:27) "And He uprooted them from upon their land with anger, wrath, and great fury, and He cast them to another land like this day," and it says (Yirmiya 15:2) "And it will be when they say to you, 'Where and for what will we go out?' you shall say to them, 'So says Hashem: Whoever is destined for death by plague will be for such a death, and whoever for the sword will be for the sword, and whoever for famine will be for famine, and whoever

for captivity will be for captivity," and it says (Amos 7:17) *"So says Hashem: Your wife will commit immorality in the city, and your sons and daughters will fall by the sword, and your land will be divided by the measuring rope, and you will die upon an impure land, and Israel will surely be exiled from upon its land,"* and it says (Yirmiya 22:10) *"Do not cry for the dead, and do not shake your head in mourning for him. Surely cry for the one who is going, for he will not return ever again and see the land of his birth."*

"Don't cry for the dead": This is Yehoyakim, king of Yehuda. What is said about him? (Yirmiya 22:19) *"He will be buried as a donkey is buried."*

"Surely cry for the one who is going": This is Yehoyachin, king of Yehuda. What is said about him? (Yirmiya 52:33-34) *"His prison garments were exchanged...and his meals [were given to him always from the king, every day.]"* We learn from here that the corpse of Yehoyakim, king of Yehuda, which was cast to the dry heat by day and the frost at night, was more desirable than the life of Yehoyachin, king of Yehuda, whose throne was placed above the throne of the other kings, and who ate and drank in the palaces of kings.

The Midrash teaches us a couple of very clear lessons:

1) Physical exile from Eretz Yisrael was and remains the worst punishment Hashem could bring upon the Jewish people.

2) A life in exile with great honor, free from material concerns, is a greater punishment than death without dignity in Eretz Yisrael. No material compensation can make up for being exiled from Eretz Yisrael.

In other words, no Jew in his right mind would leave Eretz Yisrael for *galus* for all the money and honor in the world.

This is further illustrated by the Sifrei on Devarim 12:29 (cited earlier by the Ramban on Sefer HaMitzvos):

"וירשת אותם וישבת" מעשה ברבי יהודה בן בתירה ורבי מתיה בן חרש ורבי חנניה בן אחי רבי יהושע ורבי יונתן שהיו יוצאים חוצה לארץ והגיעו לפלטום וזכרו את ארץ ישראל. זקפו עיניהם וזלגו דמעותיהם וקרעו בגדיהם וקראו את המקרא הזה (שם יא:לא) "וירשתם אותה וישבתם בה ושמרתם לעשות את כל החקים האלה" אמרו ישיבת ארץ ישראל שקולה כנגד כל המצוות שבתורה.

מעשה ברבי אלעזר בן שמוע ורבי יוחנן הסנדלר שהיו הולכים לנציבים

אצל רבי יהודה בן בתירה ללמוד ממנו תורה, והגיעו לצײדן וזכרו את ארץ ישראל. זקפו עיניהם וזלגו דמעותיהם וקרעו בגדיהם וקראו את המקרא הזה (שם) "וירשתם אותה וישבתם בה ושמרת לעשות את כל החוקים האלה ואת המשפטים" אמרו ישיבת ארץ ישראל שקולה כנגד כל המצוות שבתורה. חזרו ובאו להם לארץ ישראל.

"And you shall drive them out and settle [in their land]." It happened with Rabbi Yehuda ben Beseira, Rabbi Masya ben Charash, Rabbi Chananya the nephew of Rabbi Yehoshua, and Rabbi Yonasan, who were going out to Chutz La'aretz, that they reached Paltom, and they remembered Eretz Yisrael. They lifted their eyes, their tears flowed, they tore their clothing, and read this verse (Devarim 11:31): "And you shall inherit it and settle in it and take care to do all of these laws." And they said, Living in Eretz Yisrael weighs as much as all the mitzvos in the Torah.

It happened with Rabbi Elazar ben Shamua and Rabbi Yochanan the shoemaker, who were going to Netzivim to learn Torah from Rabbi Yehuda ben Beseira, that they reached Tzidon and remembered Eretz Yisrael. They lifted their eyes, their tears flowed, they tore their clothing, and read this verse: "And you shall inherit it and settle in it and take care to do all of these laws and statutes." They said, Living in Eretz Yisrael weighs as much as all the mitzvos in the Torah. They turned back and came back to Eretz Yisrael.

The latter sages had one of the best "excuses" to leave Eretz Yisrael — to learn Torah from one of the greatest teachers of the generation. Nevertheless, they could not bear to forsake the land, and consoled themselves with the knowledge that whatever *mitzvos* they sacrificed were more than made up for by remaining in Eretz Yisrael.

How can any Jew casually dismiss the tremendous spiritual weight of living in Eretz Yisrael, which remains true irrespective of the epoch in history?

Like a portion in the world to come

Bereishis 33:19 describes in detail that Yaacov purchased a portion of a field in Shechem where he pitched his tent. Ibn Ezra explains the significance of this seemingly minor transaction:

והזכיר זה הכתוב להודיע כי מעלה גדולה יש לארץ ישראל, ומי שיש לו בה חלק, חשוב הוא כחלק עולם הבא.

And the scripture mentioned this to make it known that there is a great advantage to the Land of Israel, and one who has a portion in it, it is considered like a portion in the world to come.

It's difficult to permit leaving Eretz Yisrael even for a mitzvah

The Gemara in Yerushalmi Shevi'is 16b demonstrates the great *halachic* and spiritual implications of leaving Eretz Yisrael:

רבי יסא שמע דאתת אימיה לבוצרה שאל לרבי יוחנן מהו לצאת אמר ליה אם מפני סכנת דרכים צא אם משום כבוד אמך איני יודע אמר רב שמואל בר רב יצחק עוד היא צריכא לרבי יוחנן אטרח עלוי ואמר גמרתה לצאת תבוא בשלום שמע רבי לעזר ומר אין רשות גדולה מזו.

> Rabbi Yossi heard that his mother had come to Botzra. He asked Rabbi Yochanan, "May I go out [of Eretz Yisrael to meet her]?" He said to him, "If it is because of danger on the roads, go out. If it is for the sake of honoring your mother, I don't know."
> Rav Shmuel bar Rav Yitzchak said, Rabbi Yochanan is still unsure [whether it is permitted]. He [Rabbi Yossi] burdened him, and he [Rabbi Yochanan] said, "You have made up your mind to go out. Come in peace."
> Rabbi Elazar heard this and said, There is no greater permission than this.

The commentaries explain that Rabbi Yossi had a particular *halachic* issue because he was a Kohen, and Kohanim are normally prohibited by rabbinic decree to leave Eretz Yisrael. Although Rabbi Yochanan ultimately gave his consent, it is clear that it was no small matter.

The Gemara in Bavli Kiddushin 31b adds further details to the story. After Rabbi Yossi left Eretz Yisrael, he learned that his mother had already passed away, and she was coming in a coffin.

Upon hearing this he remarked:

אי ידעי לא נפקי.

"Had I known I would not have left."

The insanity of leaving Eretz Yisrael

The Gemara in Kesubos 110b-112b is filled with teachings that emphasize the great importance of living in Eretz Yisrael. A story is related on 111a:

ההוא גברא דנפלה ליה יבמה בי חוזאה אתא לקמיה דרבי חנינא אמר ליה מהו למיחת וליבמה? אמר ליה אחיו נשא כותית ומת ברוך המקום שהרגו והוא ירד אחריו.

A yevama fell to a certain man in Bei Choza'ah. He came before Rabbi Chanina and said to him, "Am I allowed to go down (out of Eretz Yisrael) and marry her through yibum?" He said to him, "His brother married a Cuthite and died. Blessed is Hashem for killing him! And he should go down after him?!"

Later on the page we have a similar teaching:

אילפא מוסיף בה דברים מעשה באחד שהיה מצטער על אשה אחת וביקש לירד כיון ששמע כזאת גלגל בעצמו עד יום מותו.

Ilfa further added [to the previous teachings denigrating being in Chutz La'aretz.] It happened with a person who was pained over a woman [in Chutz La'aretz, who he desired to marry], and he sought to go down. Once he heard [teachings] like these he restrained himself until the day he died.

It's remarkable that the one source that is commonly distorted to go against this clear and consistent position of Chazal — the Gemara about the oaths — also appears on this page. The restrictive oaths are surrounded by numerous sources emphasizing the great importance of living in Eretz Yisrael, irrespective of the epoch in history. It should be clear that the teaching about the oaths is not coming to contradict all the surrounding teachings, which provide overwhelming evidence of Chazal's position on Eretz Yisrael versus Chutz La'aretz, but simply to restrict us from trying to force the redemption, as we discussed at length.

Contradicting our own prayers

For the Jewish people to be physically exiled from their land is a tremendous humiliation and desecration of Hashem's name. One of the many sources that illustrates this is Yoel 2:17, when the Jewish people were threatened with a famine in Eretz Yisrael:

בין האולם ולמזבח יבכו הכהנים משרתי ה' ויאמרו חוסה ה' על עמך ואל תתן נחלתך לחרפה למשל בם גוים למה יאמרו בעמים איה אלהיהם.

Between the auditorium and the altar let the Kohanim, Hashem's ministers, cry and say, "Have compassion, Hashem, on Your people! Do not deliver Your inheritance to humiliation, for the nations to rule over it. Why should they say among the peoples 'Where is their God?'"

In the Monday and Thursday *tachanun* we beseech Hashem with these very words to bring us out of *galus*. Are we paying attention to what we are saying? How can we expect Hashem to react to our prayers if our actions contradict them, and we spurn the opportunity to leave *galus* that He mercifully granted us?

Radak elaborates:

כי כשהיה רעב בארץ ישראל היו יוצאים רבים ממנה לגור בארץ מצרים ובארץ פלשתים מפני הרעב וזה היה חרפה להם ומושלים בהם גוים בהיותם גרים בארצם.

For when there was a famine in Eretz Yisrael many would go out from it to live in the land of Egypt and the land of the Plishtim due to the famine. This was a great humiliation for them, and the nations would rule over them while they lived in their land.

The nations of the world naturally view the exile of the Jewish people as evidence that "their God" is nonexistent or has abandoned them. This is the ultimate *chillul* Hashem.

It is also a humiliation for Jews to be ruled over by other nations, which naturally comes with living in foreign lands. Even if Jews in *galus* are granted a measure of freedom, independence, and even self-governance, they are nevertheless under the rule of the host nation.

The Jewish nation cannot fulfill its potential and ultimate purpose in exile — only with full independence and autonomy in Eretz Yisrael. Therefore, it is unthinkable that large numbers of "religious" Jews would choose to remain in exile for the reasons that have become socially and religiously acceptable in our time. This is literally choosing to prolong and exacerbate the ultimate *chillul* Hashem and humiliation of the Jewish people.

Some even argue that Jews who live in Eretz Yisrael before Moshiach comes are not allowed to govern themselves, but must seek out *goyim* to rule over the land. This is perverse! We have seen extensively that the redemption process begins with a mass return *before* Moshiach comes. Are we supposed to ask the gentiles we invited to rule over us to kindly step aside once Moshiach arrives? Are we supposed to rebel against them through no fault of their own? Is there a wealth of Torah sources supporting *that*?

Even though we are warned not to try to force the redemption, there is nothing wrong with the millions of Jews in Eretz Yisrael governing themselves. That's precisely what we are supposed to do in Eretz Yisrael, whenever we are fortunate enough to have the opportunity — with or without Moshiach!

Furthermore, there is nothing wrong with a self-governing community of Jews in Eretz Yisrael defending themselves from enemies, and organizing for that purpose. Although the IDF has proven to be anything but an authentic Jewish army, in principle we have every right and obligation to defend ourselves in our land (or, for that matter, wherever we are under threat).

Unfortunately many people have conflated the above positions — which are fully supported by the Torah and grounded in basic common sense — with supporting the Erev Rav Zionist establishment. This has led to great confusion, needless rifts among the Jewish people, tremendous *chillul* Hashem, and set back the redemption process. Greater knowledge and understanding of the Torah's teachings will hopefully turn this around.

It's not supposed to be easy

We have seen the great importance of the Jewish people returning to Eretz Yisrael, both on a personal level and en masse, the latter being a necessary precursor to the coming of Moshiach. In light of this, it is no wonder that there is a *yetzer hara* like no other for Jews to remain in *galus*. The spiritual impediments are commensurate with the rewards.

As the Gemara in Brachos 5a teaches:

תניא רבי שמעון בן יוחאי אומר שלש מתנות טובות נתן הקדוש ברוך הוא לישראל וכולן לא נתנן אלא ע״י יסורין אלו הן תורה וארץ ישראל והעולם הבא.

We learned in a Baraysa, Rabbi Shimon ben Yochai said, Hashem gave three good gifts to Israel, and all of them were only given through affliction. These are the three: Torah, Eretz Yisrael, and the world to come.

It's not supposed to be easy.

The yetzer hara *to remain in* galus

This *yetzer hara* to remain in *galus* manifests itself in the sheer number and variety of arguments/excuses people come up with to forsake living in Eretz Yisrael, the desperation and passion with which people cling to *galus*, as if living there weren't the worst punishment Hashem could bring upon the Jewish people short of destroying us, God forbid.

Eicha Rabba 1:29 teaches that if the Jewish people found respite in *galus* they would never leave:

> "וישלח את היונה וגו'", "ולא מצאה היונה מנוח וגו'". יהודה בר נחמן בשם ר"ש אמר אלו מצאה מנוח לא היתה חוזרת. ודכוותה (איכה א:ג) "היא ישבה בגוים לא מצאה מנוח", אלו מצאה מנוח לא היו חוזרים. ודכוותה (דברים כח:סה) "ובגוים ההם לא תרגיע ולא יהיה מנוח וגו'", הא אלו מצאה מנוח לא היו חוזרים.

> *"And he sent away the turtledove...and the turtledove did not find respite...." (Bereishis 8). Yehuda bar Nachman said in the name of Rabbi Shimon, had it found respite it would not have returned. Similarly, (Eicha 1:3) "She lived among the nations but did not find respite." Had she [the assembly of Israel] found respite, they would not return. Similarly, (Devarim 28:65) "And among these nations you will not find tranquility and will not have respite...." If she found respite they would not return.*

This is not a new phenomenon. Even the generation of the desert sought an excuse to return to *galus* and slavery. As Chazal teach in Bamidbar Rabba 7:4:

ולמה מתרעמין? אלא שהיו מבקשין עלילה האיך לחזור למצרים.

Why did they complain [about the Mann]? They were only seeking a pretext for how to return to Egypt.

After all, they had a good deal on fish, garlic, and other such items in Egypt. Today's *galus* Jews can relate to that.

The excuse of seeking a safer land

Of course, many Jews play the actuary and argue that it's much more dangerous to live in Eretz Yisrael. Strangely, they do not give paramount importance to such considerations when choosing where to live in *galus*; the largest Jewish communities tend to be in close proximity to crime-ridden areas, bastions of open anti-Semitism, and moral decay.

Suddenly they have *bitachon* that Hashem will watch over them and their children. But not in Eretz Yisrael, about which the Torah says in Devarim 11:12:

ארץ אשר ה' אלוקיך דרש אתה תמיד עיני ה' אלוקיך בה מרשית השנה ועד אחרית שנה.

A land that Hashem your God pays special attention to. The eyes of Hashem your God are upon it from the beginning of the year until the end of the year.

The Gemara in Succah 53a (also see Bereishis Rabba 100:2) gives a pithy lesson to all the actuaries:

אמר רבי יוחנן, רגלוהי דבר איניש אינון ערבין ביה לאתר דמיתבעי תמן מובילין יתיה הנהו תרתי כושאי דהוו קיימי קמי שלמה (מלכים א ד:ג) אליחרף ואחיה בני שישא סופרים דשלמה הוו יומא חד חזייה למלאך המות דהוה קא עציב א"ל אמאי עציבת א"ל דקא בעו מינאי הני תרתי כושאי דיתבי הכא מסרינהו לשעירים שדרינהו למחוזא דלוז כי מטו למחוזא דלוז שכיבו למחר חזיא מלאך המות קבדח א"ל אמאי בדיחת א"ל באתר דבעו מינאי תמן שדרתינהו מיד פתח שלמה ואמר רגלוהי דבר איניש אינון ערבין ביה לאתר דמיתבעי תמן מובילין יתיה.

Rabbi Yochanan said, The feet of a person are guarantors; they bring him to whatever place he is summoned.

These two Cushites who stood before Shlomo, (Melachim I 4:3) "Elichoref and Achiya the sons of Shisha," were scribes of Shlomo. One day he saw that the Angel of Death was sad. He said to him, "Why are you sad?" He said to him, "They are telling me to take these two Cushites who are sitting here."

He [Shlomo] gave them over to demons and sent them to the district of Luz. When they reached the district of Luz they died. The following day he saw that the Angel of Death was happy. He said to him, "Why are you happy?" He said to him, "You sent them to the place where I was asked to take them."

Immediately Shlomo opened and said "The feet of a person are guarantors; they bring him to whatever place he is summoned."

The clear message of Chazal is that when we play actuary and try to outsmart the Angel of Death, we may well be outsmarting ourselves.

Three generations in Eretz Yisrael before Moshiach

There is clearly an intermediate period between when the Jews return en masse and the days of Moshiach. The Sifrei on Ha'azinu 32:14 (317) writes:

"ויאכל תנובות שדי", אלו ארבע מלכיות. "ויניקהו דבש מסלע ושמן מחלמיש צור", אלו מציקים שהחזיקו בה בארץ ישראל והם קשים להוציא מהם פרוטה כצור, שנאמר "וזיז שדי ירענה." למחר הרי ישראל יורשים נכסיהם והם עריבים עליהם כשמן וכדבש.

> "And he consumed the bounty of the fields" — these are the four kingdoms [during the period of exile]. "And he let them suckle honey from the stone and oil from the flinty rock" — these are the tyrants who seized the Land of Israel, and it is difficult to get a small coin out of them like a rock, as it says (Tehillim 80:14) "And the beasts of the field will graze on it." On the morrow Israel will inherit their possessions, and it will be delicious for them like oil and honey.

This is a fascinating source. It clearly indicates that *after* the *galus* period has basically run its course, but *before* Moshiach comes, the Jewish people will be living in Eretz Yisrael under the control of oppressors who extort them and make it very difficult for them to live. This precisely describes the period of time in which we find ourselves today.

Indeed, it will be delicious when that which is rightfully ours will be fully restored to us, with penalties and interest.

The Sifrei has more clues about this period on the following *pasuk*:

וכן אתה מוצא לפני ימות המשיח, שאין עתידים למרוד אלא מתוך אכילה ושתיה ושלוה. מה נאמר בהם? "וישמן ישורון ויבעט."

And so you find before the days of Moshiach, that they are only destined to rebel through eating, drinking, and tranquility. What does it say about them? "And Jeshurun grew fat and kicked."

And later in the same source:

"שמנת עבית כסית", אלו שלשה דורות שלפני ימות המשיח, שנאמר (ישעיה ב:ז-ח) "ותמלא ארצו כסף וזהב...ותמלא ארצו סוסים...ותמלא ארצו אלילים."

"You grew fat, thick, covered in layers of fat" — these are three generations that precede the days of Moshiach, as it says (Yeshaya 2:7-8) "Their land is full of silver and gold, and there is no end to their treasure houses; their land is full of horses, and there is no end to their chariots; their land is full of idols [...they bow to the work of their hands, to that which their fingers made."]

These sources clearly indicate that the oppressive interlopers who rule over Eretz Yisrael before Moshiach comes will rebel against Hashem through prosperity, just like other periods in history that the Sifrei references.

Furthermore, the Jewish people will have already returned to Eretz Yisrael for at least three generations prior to the days of Moshiach, each of which will be marked by a particular type of gluttonous rebellion.

When we consider the source more deeply it gets even more interesting. The span of a generation is not precisely defined, but a reasonable approximation in our times would be 25 years. Contrary to what many of us learned in Jewish history class, the modern state of Israel was founded largely by Nazi collaborators and heretics with vicious antipathy to Torah observant Jews. They certainly fit the bill as rebelling against Hashem.

In the first 25 years of the state's existence, from 1948-1972, Israel went from being impoverished to prosperous. This generation can indeed be characterized as Israel becoming filled with silver and gold.

The second generation, roughly from 1973-1997, is noteworthy for Israel's army becoming modernized and technologically advanced. The land was filled with tanks, planes, and advanced weapons — the modern version of horses.

The third generation, roughly from 1998-2022, saw an extreme spiritual deterioration, as the Erev Rav who control the land unleashed an onslaught of immorality and perversity upon the population. In addition, they brainwashed and corrupted the people during the Covid cult with tactics reminiscent of Molech worship and other ancient idolatry. As if that's not enough, the Erev Rav began brazenly contaminating the land with Freemason, Satanic, and other idolatrous symbols on a scale far greater than ever before. Indeed, the land was filled with false gods.

It is remarkable how the first three generations of the mass return of the Jewish people to Eretz Yisrael fit with the Sifrei's characterization of the three generations of rebellion before Moshiach comes.

If our understanding of the Midrash is correct, Moshiach's arrival should be imminent. May it be Hashem's will.

It's all part of Hashem's plan

This intermediate period between the ingathering of the exiles and the coming of Moshiach is also evident from chapter 34 of Yechezkel. The chapter begins with Hashem castigating the shepherds of Israel for pasturing themselves, while neglecting the people. Hashem then promises to gather His flock from their lands of exile and return them to Israel, where they will settle in fertile dwellings (verses 1-15).

One would expect the chapter to continue with the coming of Moshiach, but there is an intermediate stage. The good shepherd, the scion of David, doesn't arrive to replace the evil shepherds until verse 23! In the interim, Hashem's sheep are ruled by larger animals who abuse their power. In verses 18 and 19 Hashem addresses these tyrants as follows:

המעט מכם המרעה הטוב תרעו ויתר מרעיכם תרמסו ברגליכם ומשקע מים תשתו ואת הנותרים ברגליכם תרפשון: וצאני מרמס רגליכם תרעינה ומרפש רגליכם תשתינה.

> *Is it too little for you that you graze on the choicest pasture, but what is left over from your grazing you trample with your feet? And you drink the clear water, then trample the rest of it with your feet [and make it muddy]? And My flock — they must graze on what your feet trampled, and drink your leftover muddy water?*

Hashem then promises to judge between the fat animals and the lean sheep, who were pushed, gored, and scattered. Only after these animals are judged, and Hashem rescues His flock from them as well, does Hashem establish the scion of David to shepherd His flock.

This prophecy has been partially fulfilled in our time. After thousands of years of Eretz Yisrael being desolate and under foreign occupation, millions of Jews have returned to Eretz Yisrael, which blossomed for them as it did for no one else. However, Hashem's flock is being dominated by stronger animals from among them. These gangsters seize the best for themselves, which is bad enough, but then they treat the weaker sheep with disdain, spoiling what they leave over purely out of spite.

The modern State of Israel has historically had two classes — those with special privileges, and those who suffer mightily just to get by. This is not because Hashem didn't bless the land and the people, but because the fat animals seized control of everything and pushed the sheep aside. Still, the sheep managed to get along and were generally content.

Now it's different. The fat animals — the Erev Rav gangsters who rule the land — have embraced the globalist plan to control resources, create shortages, and destroy people's ability to make ends meet. They force people out of work, force businesses into bankruptcy, impose massive fines for breathing normally [*note: this section was originally written during the Covid era*], raise taxes even more, give a raise to their cronies, then sneer that it's all for our own good. They surveil us, spy on us, rob us of our liberty, turn us into lab rats, and wage psychological warfare on us to keep us in line.

They demand we choose our form of persecution and death — bioweapon injection, or political, economic, and social strangulation.

They fatten themselves on the best pasture, then leave filthy, insufficient leftovers for the feeble sheep.

There is clearly an intermediate period of internal oppression before Moshiach comes. Hashem brings us back to Israel — yes, He wanted us to return before Moshiach comes — and then He has to save us from the animals in our midst. This is the period in which we find ourselves.

This was all foretold thousands of years ago. No one knows how much longer this period will last, but it seems unlikely that it can go on for much longer. Hashem will step in, judge the fat animals, and establish the scion of David as our righteous shepherd.

This straightforward prophecy from Yechezkel is speaking directly to us, and should strengthen us in these difficult times. It's all part of the plan, and it's all under control. We need to pray for Hashem to judge our oppressors, free us from their grip, and restore the kingdom of David under Torah law.

What we should not do, however, is miss or misinterpret the clear signs that Hashem wants us to return to Eretz Yisrael, thereby prolonging the *galus* and all that comes with it, God forbid.

Distinguished children

The Gemara in Shevi'is 15b records a dispute between Rabbi Elazar and Rabbi Yossi bar Chanina. Rabbi Elazar holds that *ma'aser* during the Bayis Sheni period was obligatory only by rabbinic decree, while Rabbi Yossi bar Chanina holds that the obligation was from the Torah itself, as in previous times.

Rabbi Elazar cites a *pasuk* which seems to indicate that the Jews who returned to Eretz Yisrael accepted the *mitzvah* of *ma'aser* on their own; in other words, via rabbinic decree. Rabbi Yossi bar Chanina explains the *pasuk* as follows:

מכיון שקיבלו עליהן בסבר פנים יפות העלה עליהן הכתוב כאילו מאיליהן.

Since they accepted it [the Torah commandment] upon themselves with a pleasant disposition, the scripture considers it as if it was on their own.

Rabbi Shlomo Sirilio explains:

כמו בנים שחוזרים לבית אביהם בלא קריאת אביהם דחשיבי מאותן דאינן חוזרים אלא בקריאה כן היו שמחים בקבלת המצוות כאילו לא עבר עליהן שמד ולא גרוש של נבוכדנצר.

Like children who return to their father's house without being called by their father, who are more distinguished than those who don't return unless they are called, so they were happy in accepting the mitzvos as if neither the destruction nor the exile of Nevuchadnetzar had come upon them.

The metaphor is striking, especially considering the tepid response of the *galus* Jews at the time when the opportunity to return home dangled before them. Surely then as well there were many who missed and misinterpreted the clear signs that Hashem wanted them to return, who made excuses great and small, who conjured up creative, intellectually dishonest Torah arguments, or who otherwise refused to leave *galus* unless their Father in Heaven called them in a way no one could deny.

Unfortunately, they missed the point and squandered the opportunity, the consequences of which we suffer to this day.

Children who return to their father's house without being called are more distinguished than those who wait for an engraved invitation.

The Torah sources and teachings from Chazal throughout the ages are clear and consistent. Let us shake free of the *yetzer hara* to remain in *galus* and stop prolonging it, once and for all.

Afterword

A very modest Rav from Yerushalayim who reviewed the *sefer* offered many helpful comments and corrections, and suggested several Torah sources that I incorporated.

He also shared the following "supplement" to his comments, which is a fitting conclusion to the *sefer*. It should be noted that he does not identify in any way with modern "Zionism." Here are his words:

There is an important point concerning "Aliyah" to Eretz Yisrael which I feel should be emphasized, and is most definitely the main intention of the numerous מאמרי חז"ל [statements of our Sages] which you've brought.

A person who makes Aliyah, especially if the move was difficult, will rightfully feel he has done something of great importance for himself, his future descendants, and for Klal Yisrael. But it might be in his own eyes a peak he has successfully reached, and now can retire. He might continue his life without much effort to rise even higher in his Torah-learning, accurate strict *mitzvah* observance, character improvement, and steadfast devotion to the will of Hashem in every aspect of life. After all, this person has done so much already in his רוחניות [spirituality].

In truth, this person has climbed, but merely to a plateau, not to his peak.

There are but four לשונות של גאולה [terms of redemption], namely והוצאתי והצלתי וגאלתי ולקחתי, of which the fourth, ולקחתי, refers to מתן תורה at הר סיני [the giving of the Torah at Mount Sinai] (see Seforno Shemos 6:6-7). The following promise, והבאתי, isn't another לשון גאולה, but a precious gift from Hashem to assist Klal Yisrael to properly observe the Torah mentioned in

ולקחתי, a land which elevates those who seek elevation. Eretz Yisrael isn't an end of its own, but rather a big step forward, and upward, in one's perpetual spiritual Aliyah, striving evermore to achieve greater levels of Torah, Mitzvos, and Avodas Hashem. This Aliyah is hard to successfully achieve anywhere, but easier in Eretz Yisroel than anywhere else.

Therefore, encouragement to make Aliyah should be coupled with the revelation that Eretz Yisroel is a <u>gold-mine</u> of רוחניות, and is there for the taking. Aliyah to Eretz Yisroel shouldn't end upon arrival; it should continue on and on, in Aliyah of רוחניות. Just as there is no acceptable excuse for not making Aliyah <u>to</u> Eretz Yisroel, because it is available, so too there is no acceptable excuse for not making Aliyah <u>in</u> Eretz Yisroel, because it is available to one and all. And Hashem wants it.

This concept should be emphasized. It is inspiring! Until here are the holy words of the Rav.

Indeed, we have no reason to be in Eretz Yisrael *except* to keep the Torah both individually and as a society. This is why the land was given to us, and this is why Hashem, in His great mercy, gave us the opportunity to return in large numbers after so many bitter years estranged from our land.

A physical return to Eretz Yisrael is a critical step forward in our personal and national development, but it is only a beginning. We must not become complacent and satisfied. We must yearn for truly Jewish leadership, composed strictly of God-fearing, Torah-minded people, who will oversee the implementation of Torah as the law of the land.

When enough of us truly want this, Hashem will surely not deny us. May it be soon in our days.

Appendix

Go Up Like a Wall, Chapter 14: Returning Like a Wall

Before we proceed to the Book of Zecharya, we must address a critical loose end: a loaded phrase used by the Malbim in his introduction to Chagai. The Malbim asserted that the return to Israel was originally intended to recharge the spiritual batteries of the nation to prepare them for prolonged exile, as the spiritual state of the people had rapidly deteriorated to perilous levels in the short span of 70 years. However, this return to Israel brought with it many of the ingredients necessary for the ultimate redemption. This created the potential for the Jews to "cheat" their way out of exile and turn this emergency interruption of the exile into the ultimate redemption.

This potential would have been fulfilled, writes the Malbim, "if they returned in full repentance to Hashem and all made *aliya* like a wall [en masse]." The phrase "making *aliya* like a wall" is a key phrase in a most controversial *drasha*, and is deliberately used by the Malbim to call this *drasha* to mind.

It is found in two places, the Gemara in Ketubot (111a) and the Midrash on Shir HaShirim (2:7, page 32 in the Vilna edition). In the former source it is cited by Rav Zeira in defense of his plan to make *aliya*, which was challenged by Rav Yehuda. Rav Zeira defended himself by saying that it is only forbidden for the Jews to return to Israel "like a wall" (until the time of the redemption). Rashi explains this to mean "en masse, by force."

In the Midrash on Shir HaShirim this source is cited by Rabbi Chelbo, where the teaching is discussed in more detail. It states as follows:

"Rabbi Yossi bar Chanina said, There are two oaths here, one for Israel and one for the nations of the world. [Hashem] swore regarding Israel that they should not rebel against the yoke of the kingdoms [in their exile], and He swore regarding the nations of the world that they should not place a heavy yoke on Israel. For if they place a heavy yoke on Israel they cause the end to come [before] its designated time . . .

"Rabbi Chelbo says there are four oaths here [four verses in Shir HaShirim mention an oath]. He swore regarding Israel that they should not rebel against the kingdoms; that they should not force the end [other versions: distance the end {through their sins}]; that they should not reveal their secrets [of the Torah] to the nations of the world; and that they should not go up like a wall from the exile.

"If so, why will the King Moshiach come? To gather the exiles of Israel. "Rabbi Oniah said, The four oaths correspond to four generations that forced the end and stumbled . . . "

This Midrash is commonly referenced and grossly misinterpreted by numerous supposedly Torah-observant Jews to justify antagonism against modern-day Israel and to discourage Jews from making *aliya*. As is typical of those who engage in agenda-based citations of Torah sources, they conveniently quote only that which — taken in a vacuum — supports their agenda. The rest of the source either doesn't exist, or is interpreted in a way that renders it meaningless — all while they magnify the snippet that suits their agenda out of context and out of proportion. Their agenda is thus branded as inviolable, unquestionable Torah truth, and all who fail to fall into step are branded enemies of the Torah.

Let us examine what the Midrash is really teaching us.

Rabbi Yossi bar Chanina teaches that the period of exile is based on a symbiotic relationship between the Jews and the nations of the world. The Jews are expected to accept the authority of the nations during their exile and remain loyal to their hosts. In return, the nations of the world are expected to refrain from treating the Jews in a heavy-handed fashion.

(I purposely do not write that the Jews and the nations "swore" to do this, as virtually anyone who references this Midrash will phrase it, because that is not consistent with the wording of the Midrash. Who actually took this oath? When did they take it?

The Midrash consistently states that Hashem swore regarding others, which is another way of saying that the content of the oaths indicate His definite will. Even those who would claim that some unnamed representatives of the Jewish people literally took such an oath, they would be hard pressed to make this same claim regarding the nations of the world, and the phraseology is consistent in all cases. The lesson of the Midrash might be the same, but it is far more powerful to be able to claim "the Jews swore not to make *aliya*" than to say "Hashem doesn't want the Jews to return to Israel as a nation under most circumstances.")

The Yefe Kol commentary spells out the consequences of this relationship between the Jews in exile and their host nations: if the nations treat the Jews in heavy-handed fashion, they will cause the redemption to come before its designated time.

This is an entirely rational concept. The exile is a punishment to expiate the sins of the nation.

The duration of the exile is designated, barring certain factors that can either hasten the redemption (such as mass repentance) or, God forbid, delay it (such as mass corruption). One such factor that can hasten the redemption is if the nations of the world oppress the Jews far beyond what is considered "reasonable." For one thing, oppressing the Jews drastically accelerates the process of expiating the sins of the nation, and therefore reduces the period of exile. In addition, by oppressing the Jews the nations show themselves unworthy of the authority given them, they pile up sins on their own accounts, and they arouse God's love for His nation. (See also Yeshaya 14:1 and Malbim, which is another example of Hashem expressing that He will redeem the Jews out of mercy.)

This concept is universally accepted regarding the redemption from Egypt, which occurred after 210 years (only a relatively small part of which consisted of slavery), as opposed to the 400 years that had been decreed upon the Jews. Hashem factored in the "quality" of the exile to reduce the duration of the exile.

Far from categorically forbidding mass *aliya*, the teaching of Rabbi Yossi bar Chanina strongly indicates that modern Israel is God's will. It is no coincidence that the State was born on the heels of the most heinous oppression of the Jewish people since the destruction of Jerusalem. It is no coincidence that this rather heavy-handed treatment of the Jews precipitated the greatest moment of redemption since the destruction of Jerusalem.

Ideally this redemption would have occurred under more favorable circumstances, but to deny that it was God's doing and God's will because it was not accompanied by a mass *teshuva* movement and King Moshiach riding in on his horse is simply ignorant. To further support this ignorant claim by dissevering the second half of Rabbi Yossi bar Chanina's words is disingenuous.

Rabbi Chelbo derives four oaths from the text of Shir HaShirim, and applies them all to Israel.

The first is that they should not rebel against the kingdoms, which we can understand plainly as accepting their authority while in exile.

The second is that they should not force the end, which means to raise an army and wage war against the nations to fight their way out of exile. This explanation is proven by the immediately following examples of the four generations which went against this expression of God's will, and were unsuccessful.

It must be emphasized that this has nothing to do with defending ourselves from hostile elements. It is not Hashem's will for the nations to slaughter the Jews, nor for the Jews to meekly submit to slaughter — even if our sins cause divine protection to be removed, God forbid. Another version of the Midrash changes one letter of this oath, which completely alters the meaning. Instead of reading "yidchaku" this version reads "yirchaku," which means the Jews should not distance the redemption by piling sins onto those which already need to be expiated. (This version also clearly indicates that these "oaths" are not oaths that actual human beings formally took, but expressions of God's definite will, as we explained.)

The third oath, that we should not reveal secrets of the Torah to the nations, is interesting, but not relevant to our discussion.

The fourth oath contains the key phrase with which we began: that they should not go up like a wall from the exile. This is also explained as an act of rebellion against the nations and, by extension, the exile that had been decreed upon the nation.

But what if the nations encouraged the Jews to make *aliya*?

What if the forced exile was over and the only thing holding the Jews back from leaving was their willingness to pack their bags and go? Clearly the intention of the Midrash is not to prohibit a mass return to Israel until Moshiach forcibly drags the Jews onto a plane.

Indeed, the very next line of the Midrash questions the purpose of Moshiach. He is not a rescuer who parachutes into the teeth of the exile and extracts hostage Jews. Rather, his job is to gather those who have refrained from returning before he arrived. One of the commentaries on the page even speculates that this a derogatory statement about the exiles who require Moshiach to bring them back.

After all, once the exile is over, what Jew in his right mind would remain there one moment longer? What Jew in his right mind would prefer to continue a state of existence that was decreed as the worst of national punishments?

It is no coincidence indeed that the Malbim writes that the second Beit Hamikdash could have been the ultimate redemption if the exiles returned like a wall. The Malbim understood this Midrash quite well, and thus understood that returning en masse was only contrary to God's will when done by force against the nations of the world while the period of exile was still clearly in effect. When Koresh, the King of Persia, gave his instruction and blessing for the Jews to return to Israel en masse, taking him up on that could hardly be considered an act of rebellion or a violation of God's will. His words signaled the end of the exile period. It then became *incumbent* upon the Jews to make *aliya* en masse.

As if this is not powerful enough, the following Gemara in Yoma (9b) drives the point home in the sharpest of terms: "Reish Lakish was swimming in the Jordan River. Rabba bar bar Chana extended him a hand. [Reish Lakish refused to take his hand.] He said, 'By God, I hate you! As it is written 'If it is a wall, we will build for it a palace of silver, and if it is a door, we will affix it with boards of cedar' (Shir HaShirim 8:9). Had you made yourselves like a wall and all gone up in the days of Ezra, you would have been compared to silver, which does not rot. Now that you went up like doors [Rashi: like one person opening and another person closing, meaning that the Jews made *aliya* only partially] you were compared to cedar, which is liable to rot.'"

Many generations after the destruction of the second Beit Hamikdash, the descendants of the Jews of Israel harbored a burning resentment toward the descendants of those who remained in Persia. Reish Lakish declared that God hates them! Rashi explains: "God hates all the Jews of Bavel, for they did not ascend in the days of Ezra, and they prevented the *shechina* [God's presence] from coming and returning to settle on the second Beit Hamikdash.

It cannot be stated any more clearly. The second Beit Hamikdash failed to achieve its potential as the ultimate redemption because the Jewish people failed to return en masse when the opportunity was given to them.

On the heels of the Holocaust, once again the nations of the world voted to permit the Jews' return to Israel. This event was no less miraculous than the King of Persia having a similar divine inspiration, and it officially heralded the end of the prolonged exile period. Once the Jewish people are no longer compelled to remain in exile, they are expected and obligated to leave it. Doing so en masse is a vital step toward ushering in the complete redemption. Failing to do so risks squandering the opportunity and incurring God's wrath, as expressed by Reish Lakish.

Indeed, in our time the Jewish people have largely failed just as our ancestors did. And just like our ancestors did, we have experienced continuous difficulties and setbacks in resettling the land. The nations of the world have been repenting their miraculous, divinely-induced vote at the United Nations ever since that day — just as their predecessors did in the days of Ezra. Their support for the Jewish enterprise has become lukewarm at best, and is often mere camouflage.

That at any point in history the majority of world powers could vote for the creation of a Jewish state in our ancestral land is a miracle on par with any other in history — one that merits getting the message and returning en masse. Hashem's continued miraculous protection over Israel in spite of itself is further sign that He wants this return to succeed.

There are not two legitimate sides to this issue. Anyone who believes that a mass return to Israel is anything other than God's definite will is ignorant, and bears responsibility for setting back the redemption process.

If you are reading this outside of Israel, please pack your bags and return home.

If you are reading this in Israel but do not recognize or support the state as an expression of God's will, you are terribly misguided. There are many, many faults and shortcomings of the state in its current form. Nevertheless, God wants the entire nation to return and participate in the building of the state. In so doing we will help usher in the complete redemption we are all waiting for.

Why God Chose the Early Zionists

One of the most troubling theological questions of modern times is why the return to Israel was spearheaded predominantly by non-religious and even anti-religious Jews. This question is not just an intellectual mystery; it has broad implications for how religious Jews relate to and engage with the current state of Israel, which continues to have an uneasy relationship with Judaism.

Many Torah observant Jews have concluded that the ultimate redemption can't possibly occur in this fashion, and therefore reject the return to Israel as a religiously significant development. Even those who embrace the state as "the first flowering of the redemption" struggle to reconcile the continued ambivalent — at times hostile — actions of the government toward religious sectors and movements that promote Torah observance as inseparable from Jewish nationhood.

The most extreme manifestation of this is some members of the Neturei Karta sect of Jews, who align themselves with Israel's most savage enemies in seeking its destruction, all in the perverse name of performing God's will and undoing the work of Satan. Thankfully their influence is minimal; their appearance as "ultra-Orthodox" Jews provides fodder for the media, which gobbles up any opportunity to portray all religious Jews as extremists or fools by association, but it seems their value as useful idiots is confined to that. This small sect of deranged traitors is an embarrassment and a desecration of God's name, but not worthy of serious attention.

Many Orthodox Jews (typically referred to as haredi — but I am against the use of labels and categories, as they needlessly divide us based on arbitrary, often dubious externals) are indeed convinced that the ultimate redemption cannot blossom from the work of the early Zionists. However, they are at a loss to provide a plausible explanation for how and why Israel continues to grow and prosper more than 120 years later if this is indeed against God's will.

Surely there are many prolonged historical situations that we cannot fully explain — we need look no further than 2,000 years of exile and persecution. The difference is that Israel could not possibly have grown and thrived — let alone existed altogether — for so long without God's continuous miraculous intervention. If this were something that went against His will, He would simply need to look the other way for a short time and that would be the end of it, God forbid.

Despite this clear evidence that God supports the existence of Israel, for all its warts and imperfections, hard-core "haredim" seek to disassociate themselves from the state as much as possible and reject the secular Zionists as agents of God's will. It has become dogmatic for them, an inviolable belief tantamount to the Rambam's Thirteen Principles of Faith, and a prerequisite for acceptance into many of their communities. This extreme social pressure keeps people in line who would otherwise have a much more favorable view of historical developments, but are otherwise attracted to the lifestyle in these communities. It's most unfortunate and against Torah principles for a perspective on an ambiguous matter to be imposed on people this way — yet this is how much of the so-called "Torah world" operates.

If you ask someone from this camp for the proper religious approach to the Holocaust, they will respond that we have to accept it as God's perfect will, even though we cannot fathom His ways. This is a proper response. Yet, in a most bizarre irony, these same people cannot accept the return to Israel of millions of Jews under Jewish leadership — unworthy as this leadership may be — as God's will! We can accept thousands of years of destruction and persecution as God's will, but the rebuilding of Israel is the work of Satan?! Only a clever Jewish mind can contort itself to rationalize such an absurd conclusion. If anything is the work of Satan, it is that.

The rest of religious Jewry is openly supportive of the modern state, with varying degrees of ambivalence. On the extreme end of this spectrum we find religious Jews who are so ebullient about supporting Israel that they are unwilling to criticize the government. Most likely this is an over-reaction to the anti-state crowd, who will never express support for the government, as opposed to a thought-out position. It is not a rational theological approach; no one short of a prophet acting on God's clear instructions deserves a blank check — certainly not a government composed of nothing resembling divine actors. This group of religious Jews cannot explain why God chose the early Zionists, but they prefer to ignore the issue, for better or for worse.

Then we have everyone else. They firmly believe that Israel is "the real thing," but they are befuddled by Israel's identity complex. There is a clear dichotomy between how Israel should look if it were guided by true Torah leadership and how it looks today, with a seemingly insurmountable chasm between reality and this vision, which itself is murky.

The fact that Israel started as a clearly secular entity that made some room for religion, and has continued to marginalize Judaism as a personal choice — rather than part and parcel of who we are as a nation — creates a deep internal tension. "We support Israel, we love Israel… but there is something fundamentally wrong with Israel from the very moment it was re-established, and we don't know how to reconcile that." It is no surprise that many religious Jews vacillate between the opposite extremes of supporting Israel and rejecting it, and if they don't, their children do. There is no clear comfort zone.

This tension is also one of the main impediments or excuses for the many thousands of religious Jews across the world who choose to remain behind in foreign lands. This is perhaps the greatest consequence of this theological issue remaining unresolved. As long as it is not abundantly clear that the early Zionists were in fact agents of God, it is convenient for these Jews to overlook modern Israel as being God's will, and taking the logical step of fully participating in its development.

With this backdrop in mind, I will present four explanations for why the non-religious and anti-religious Zionists were not only agents of God's will, but the redemption could not possibly have occurred without them specifically orchestrating the return to Zion. Two of these explanations come from the monumental sefer, Eim Habanim Semeichah by Rav Yissachar Shlomo Teichtal, HY"D, and two are based on my own understanding of the subsequent history as it has unfolded.

All of these explanations are complementary and interrelated. Together they form a compelling argument for accepting and embracing the modern state of Israel as God's will, an unmistakable harbinger of the ultimate redemption in progress, and a divine call to world Jewry to return home to their motherland.

In Eim Habanim Semeichah (Chap. 2, Sec. 12), Rav Teichtal addresses the troubling question of how and why the secular Zionists could play such a vital role in the redemption process. He begins by stating the ultimate answer: we cannot possibly understand all of God's ways, and we must accept the fact that sometimes He chooses agents that are not palatable to us, for reasons that are beyond us. Everyone and everything is an instrument of the Divine Will, and it is not our place to deny God's intervention simply because we don't like the intermediary. Consequently, we should embrace the opportunity to return to Israel and work hand-in-hand with even the worst of Jews in settling the Land.

He then cites a Gemara, which records a tradition from the Sages that the redemption will be signaled specifically by the call of impure birds, which is a reference to sinful Jews. We know from many places that when we have a tradition from the Sages we accept it even if it runs counter to logic. Being that we have an authoritative tradition that the redemption process will begin through the actions of sinful Jews, we therefore accept it as God's will.

Rav Teichtal acknowledges that this answer will not be satisfying to everyone; indeed, it requires an extremely high level of faith. How can it be that God would choose men who exhibit no vestige of Judaism to be the orchestrators of the return?

He offers two explanations, both of which are based on kabbalistic texts and conventional Torah sources. His primary explanation, which covers the bulk of the essay, is that it was necessary for the early Zionists to be secular in order to circumvent a spiritual prosecution against the redemption. The time was ripe for redemption, but the Jewish people as a nation were not worthy of being redeemed.

We know that the redemption can come with open miracles or with hidden miracles cloaked in a chain of natural events. The manner in which the redemption occurs depends on our spiritual state.

Had the return to Israel been spearheaded by the spiritual giants of the time, the Heavenly prosecution would have rightly argued that the masses did not deserve it, and the return would have been thwarted.

God therefore chose the least likely spiritual candidates to lead the return to Israel, essentially flying under the radar of our heavenly adversaries, who were fooled into thinking that this couldn't possibly be the ultimate redemption. "These people belong to us!" they said. Once the facts on the ground were already established, it was too late for them to undo the process.

Rav Teichtal gives other examples of critical redemption-oriented events occurring in a similar fashion, with a mixture of impurity to throw off the guard of those who would try to prevent them, as explained by the great kabbalists. Chief among them is the Davidic dynasty, whose very inception came about through the unflattering episode with Yehuda and Tamar, and our first redeemer, Moshe, who grew up in the house of Pharaoh. The beginning of the return to Israel after the Destruction of the First Temple followed a similar pattern.

In light of this, we should not be surprised to find the same subterfuge with the beginning of the final redemption. While this explanation is far from down-to-earth, it is well founded in Torah and tradition.

Rav Teichtal provides a supplementary explanation (Chap. 2, Sec. 18) from the Vizhnitzer Rav, who recognized the secular Zionists as spiritual descendants of the *biryonim*. These tough but spiritually empty Jews lived at the end of the Second Temple period when Jerusalem was under siege by the Romans.

The residents had enough food to hold out for many years, but the biryonim wanted to fight, believing that they could defeat the powerful Roman army. To force their way, they burned down the storehouses of food, which led to the destruction of Jerusalem.

According to this Torah giant and kabbalist, the secular Zionists were unwittingly performing a *tikkun* (repair) for their Second Temple era ancestors, rebuilding what they had destroyed and caused to be destroyed.

Let us consider two additional explanations for why God purposely chose the secular Zionists to spearhead the return to Israel.

Imagine that the leaders were the most righteous and pious of Jews. In this scenario, the early settlement is dominated by religious Jews, who naturally control the government. The secular Jews largely remain behind in foreign countries, uninspired and uninterested in living in a religious state. The religious Jews continue to build the Land and infuse the country with holiness. Eventually the Messiah comes and completes the redemption process. Before or after this time, secular Jews become impressed with what's happening in Israel, or else need to flee persecution abroad, and decide to join their religious brothers.

I like to believe that they would be warmly welcomed at that time. Recent history, however, suggests that the reception would be quite different. Most likely they would be met with an onerous list of religious demands to be granted entry, lest they upset the spiritual condition of the country.

Even religious Jews would be subjected to an inquisition of sorts to determine if they were sufficiently observant to be worthy of acceptance. What type of *kippah* do you wear? Who is your rav? What is your standard of *kashrut*? Do you daven with a *minyan* three times a day? How much Torah do you learn every day? Do you have the internet or a smartphone? Do you have a television? Do you watch movies or read secular literature? Are the women sufficiently *tzanuah*? And on and on.

I'm all for more meticulous Torah observance, but counter-intuitive as it seems, God sometimes has different priorities. Back then and still today, the main priority was bringing the Jews back to Israel en masse, irrespective of their level of observance. The spiritual return would be a gradual process following the physical return.

God in His infinite wisdom recognized that this could only be accomplished precisely with secular Zionists in control, at least initially. Despite their indifference and even antipathy toward Judaism, any Jew can return to Israel and even receive support from the government. The Jews in Boro Park, Lakewood, and Williamsburg can all come tomorrow and build more yeshivas in Israel, and no one will stand in their way. The reverse would likely not be true.

This brings us to the fourth explanation for why God chose the secular Zionists. Had the state been built primarily by religious Jews, they would claim that the state existed entirely due to their spiritual merits and their physical efforts. Even though the less religious would be admitted to the country, they would forever be looked down upon as second-class citizens who don't really deserve to be there, subsisting entirely on the merits and good graces of their more holy brethren — a concept I discuss in my book *Go Up Like a Wall* (Chap. 21).

Because the early Zionists were primarily secular, this can never happen. Even the most spiritually bankrupt Jew can forever hold his head up high for his sacrifices and contributions to the settlement of the Land, without which the redemptive process would not have been possible. This is in no way a substitute for Torah observance or an excuse for un-Jewish behavior, but it is a feather in their cap that no one can take away from them.

This is exactly the way God wanted it to be, for He loves all Jews and wants all Jews to feel their right to the Land and ownership of it. It was also the only way to ensure the potential for true unity among the entire nation, for all Jews can rightfully say that their contributions to the state are vital. Being that unity is also a prerequisite for the redemption, we can now understand in very practical terms why God purposely chose the secular Zionists. It was the way it had to be, plain and simple, both in spite of their serious flaws and because of them.

We look forward to the complete return of world Jewry to their motherland, the gradual spiritual return of the nation, and the completion of the redemption process that is already very much underway.

What Mordechai Teaches The Galus Jew

Mordechai is introduced to us in Megillas Esther as follows: "He was exiled from Jerusalem with the group of exiles that were exiled with Yechonya, king of Yehudah, whom Nevuchadnezzar, king of Bavel, exiled" (2:6).

The Vilna Gaon makes an astonishing comment based on the repetitive mentions of Mordechai's exile in this single verse: "[This is] to inform us of his love for Eretz Yisrael, for each time [he was exiled] he returned to Jerusalem, and he was exiled three times."

Mordechai lived through the gradual destruction of the original settlement of Israel, which had been forewarned for generations and whose end was by then a fait accompli. Israel was a sinking ship, both materially and spiritually, the Beis HaMikdash was all but doomed, and most of the Torah scholars were already in exile. Israel's kings were puppets without power, and the vast majority of the land was already under foreign occupation. The end was a matter of when, not if.

The "rational" thing for Mordechai to do was set up shop in Bavel with his rabbinic colleagues, build a nice *frum* community, and pray for the welfare of the government that would rule over them and hopefully not persecute them too badly.

Instead, Mordechai did just the opposite. At the very first opportunity, he turned around and returned to Israel, a trek of hundreds of miles.

It wasn't long before the situation in Israel deteriorated further. Once again, Mordechai was forcibly exiled. Once again, the moment the dust settled, he turned around and trekked back to Israel. Not long after, Mordechai was exiled for a third time, and he probably could have given directions by then. This time, there was nothing left to return to, so Mordechai became a leader of the Diaspora community, an honored member of the Persian king's court, rescued the king from an assassination attempt, taught Torah to the masses, and saved the Jews from Haman's plan to destroy them. Mordechai even managed to receive approval from most of his fellow Jews, the rarest of feats. He had it made.

Nevertheless, when the opportunity arose to return to Israel and rebuild the Jewish settlement, Mordechai left the exile once again, this time making the trek at a very advanced age. He is named as one of the men of the Great Assembly during the times of Ezra.

Mordechai single-handedly throws cold water on every justification Jews have for remaining in exile:

There was greater Torah scholarship in Bavel.

The Israeli government was anti-Orthodox, and spiritual leaders were persecuted.

Jews in Israel were in constant danger, and it was safer in exile.

The prophets had made it clear that exile had been decreed by G-d; Moshiach certainly hadn't announced his arrival.

Enemy attacks and sieges had caused famines and plagues; it was definitely easier to make a living in exile.

There was greater Jewish unity in exile.

It was definitely easier to raise children in exile.

The trek to Israel was arduous and dangerous, especially for older people.

Many rabbis were clearly in favor of remaining in exile.

Mordechai had already tried to make *aliya* multiple times, only to be forced to leave Israel again. He had every right to conclude that he was absolved, and it was G-d's will for him to remain in exile.

Mordechai had a terrific life in exile, and returning to Israel would mean lowering his standard of living in many respects. Exile was far more comfortable.

Mordechai was a vital member of the community, a leader in both the spiritual and secular worlds, and he was doing holy work in the exile.

Despite all of the above, Mordechai returned to Israel twice during the period of its downfall, and then again 70 years later when it became feasible to do so. The vast majority of Jews voluntarily remained in exile when they were no longer forced to be there for all the reasons Mordechai repeatedly dismissed. This is the main reason *Bayis Sheni* was handicapped from the very beginning and doomed to fail (see Kuzari II:24 and my sefer, *Go Up Like a Wall*). When push came to shove, most of the Jews did not truly love *Eretz Yisrael*, and they preferred to remain in exile.

Mordechai had every excuse to remain in exile, and he wanted no part of it. Mordechai never forgot what it means to be a Jew. He was forced into exile three times, but he never let the exile be forced into him. When others rationalized and compromised, Mordechai remained staunch and proud. When the gates to Israel were once again opened, Mordechai didn't hesitate or make calculations.

Returning to Israel — regardless of the challenges and sacrifices — was a no-brainer.

Today we universally recognize Mordechai as a national hero and a spiritual role model. He is introduced to us as someone who refused to live in exile when there was any opportunity to get out. If Mordechai lived today, he would be in Israel, no ifs, ands, or buts.

We celebrate his example every year. It's time to follow it.

What's Your *Galus* Exit Plan?

There is very little that we know with certainty, but one thing we do know is that at some point in the future — most likely in the relatively near future — the Jewish nation will return to Israel in its entirety. That is our destiny, a divine guarantee that has kept our people going in the darkest of times, and it is rapidly unfolding.

It's time for both individuals and entire communities to plan their exit from the exile. Like a company that is being disbanded, the time has come to wind down the *galus*, close up shop, and enter a new era. It's going to happen regardless, so best to be proactive.

Which of the following is *your* exit plan?

I only want to be buried in Israel

It might not sound like much, but this still means something. For one thing, there are cemeteries all over the world, and choosing one in Israel demonstrates an attachment to the land in the most literal sense. There is often an ulterior motive involved here. Tradition teaches that in Messianic times, when the dead come back to life, those buried outside of Israel will have to roll here through underground tunnels. This will surely be an unpleasant experience, especially if Israel blows them up, mistakenly thinking these tunnels were made by Hamas. To avoid this problem, many Jews choose to be buried in Israel. They want to reside here only as dead people, but it's something.

I am waiting for Moshiach to come

This is the exit plan of the vast majority of religious Jews who live in the Diaspora. It is similar to the plan of the dead, who are also waiting for Moshiach to come in order to live here. The latter group would likely be more exuberant upon his arrival; the former, for all their prayers, would largely find it a terribly inconvenient upheaval of their utopian religious life in exile, free of the responsibility to do more than merely survive.

Some fringe elements of the religious population have even come to believe that it is forbidden to live in Israel, or to support it in any way, until Moshiach comes. We hope Moshiach himself doesn't share this belief, since that would create quite a conundrum; if he decides to come today, must he disassociate himself from the *medina*, seek to tear it down, and then build it up again from scratch?

Hopefully he will simply become the leader of the current *medina* and bring what currently exists into the Messianic period. That would certainly be more convenient for all concerned.

Those who have adopted this exit plan must ask themselves if perhaps Moshiach is actually waiting for *them* to come, and not the other way around. Considering the way history has unfolded, it seems rather likely that this is the case.

I am waiting for retirement

This exit plan is superior to the previous ones, since it includes residing in Israel during part of one's actual life. This group chooses to spend its prime years, its working years, its youth on foreign soil. That is lamentable. But at least Israel is more than a cemetery to this group; it is a retirement community. It is an even more Jewish version of Florida. There is what to come for that is above the ground, not only below it. This includes the health-care system, tours throughout the country, lectures, and more.

Unfortunately, for the most part it does not include building and creating for the next generation, actually being part of the process. Most of the contributions of these people will be enjoyed by foreign countries. They work their whole lives for other countries and come to Israel in the twilight of their days. It's something. But that's all it is.

I am waiting until I earn enough money to support my descendants

This exit plan will surely take a long time to come to fruition, because it is hard to decide exactly how many descendants one will have, and it is appropriate to be both optimistic and err on the side of caution. In addition, once we consider expected increases in the cost of living, yeshiva tuitions, college tuitions, inflation, and putting enough money away for rainy days, that's a hefty load of cash we're talking about. Considering how hard it will be to earn quite enough even in the Golden Diaspora, moving to Israel means completely kissing that little dream goodbye.

However, once working becomes physically impossible, you can try the retirement option mentioned above, and if moving overseas at that point is also physically impossible, you can go for the burial option. At the very least, your lifetime of toil will make it possible for all your descendants to move to Israel in your stead, which surely they will do... unless you fall short of your financial goals, and they must continue your mission to earn enough money to last for all eternity.

I am waiting until I must go with only the shirt on my back

This is generally the Plan B of those with the previous exit plan, though they prefer not to phrase it in these terms. Israel is the safe haven option, if all else fails. It exists primarily so Jews will have a place to run if and when they have to run. Hopefully they will never have to run for their lives, because they don't really want to live in Israel, ever, and people shouldn't be forced to live where they don't want to be.

Historically these Jews are the ones who recognize that they are no longer especially welcome in their foreign country of choice, but wish to liquidate their assets and leave like a mensch. Unfortunately they tend to miscalculate the window for being able to leave like a mensch, and at some point will be fortunate to leave at all.

There are millions of Jews around the world today who are uncomfortable being Jewish in their foreign country of choice, much as they enjoy living there. This discomfort may involve subtle expressions of hatred for the Jew or clear and present physical dangers that they have become used to. (The ability of the Jew to become used to this is second to none.) Even Jews who do not perceive overt threats to their existence generally sense a latent threat that can become activated at any time. We've always been everyone's favorite whipping boy, nothing has changed, and we know it whether we like to admit it or not.

These millions of Jews are all waiting to book the last seat on the last El Al flight out of the country before all hell breaks loose, and do not wish to leave one minute sooner. We can only hope they are not incorrect in their prediction of when all hell will break loose, and that this last flight will not be overbooked. Jews do not have a good track record of timing these things right.

I am waiting until I get married

This is the exit plan of choice for young Jews. If they get married young, their exit plan will change to "waiting until we save up some money." Once they have kids the exit plan will change to "waiting until we save up even more money." Once they save up even more money, the exit plan will change to "waiting until it's an ideal time for us to move with our kids." This will never happen, since the burden of acclimating will always be a strong enough excuse to delay it. The exit plan will therefore change to "waiting until the children are grown and independent." Once that happens, the exit plan will change to "waiting for retirement or burial, because how can we leave our children?"

And so the cycle continues, and the exile drags on indefinitely.

I am waiting until it is safe to live in Israel

The definition of "safe" for those with this exit plan is that there is absolutely no possibility of a terrorist attack, a missile being fired, a war, or any of Israel's nearby countries ever so much as threatening Israel in a speech. It is simply unreasonable to ask a Jew to move to Israel under such circumstances. Of course, we would be horrified if all the Jews already in Israel decided to pack up and leave for exactly the same reason (though surely we would understand). Essentially, whoever is already living in Israel should show some mettle and remain to support this crazy Jewish experiment that we want to be proud of from a distance, but those who don't live there would be crazy to join it and jeopardize their lives. It is unfair to expect everyone to be a daredevil.

What's interesting about this calculus is that it's always a reasonable deal-breaker when it comes to Israel, but it never seems to be a deal-breaker when Jews move anywhere else. Jews move from communities with lower levels of crime to higher levels of crime all the time without batting an eyelash. Jews move to cities with large anti-Semitic populations, countries in Europe that are becoming increasingly Muslim-friendly and anti-Israel, places where everything that grows from the ground has Jewish blood mixed inside, and even places where it is unsafe to be recognizably Jewish. No problem. Jews will even move to Germany without a second thought. After all, they said they're sorry.

But Israel? No way. Too dangerous.

I don't know if, statistically speaking, Israel is the absolute safest place in the world for a Jew to live. It would be a great service to the Jewish people if someone can figure this out and provide ongoing updates, so Jews can choose where to live accordingly. It's all a numbers game, and giving yourself the best chance to make it to tomorrow is all that matters in life.

I am waiting until Israel is a more religious country

This is the exit plan of choice for religious Jews who don't want to admit that they are waiting for Moshiach to forcibly drag them to Israel. It always sounds nicer to contend that you would live here voluntarily, at least under some circumstances, however remote they may be.

How religious does Israel have to become for this exit plan to be activated? What does this mean exactly, and how is it to be measured? The more nebulous and unlikely the definition, the better. This is because the exit plan is never meant to be activated.

The fact is that, for all its flaws and shortcomings, Israel is right now the most religiously Jewish country in the entire world. So what, retorts the Jew in exile. The community in which I live is a utopia of religious Jewry, and I simply cannot leave it to live in a country with so much secularism (even though I live in one). I can only live in Israel if it is perfectly Torah observant, otherwise I must live in a country that is even less Torah observant. It doesn't even matter if I can find a community in Israel that is even more Torah observant than the one in which I currently live (an absolute certainty). I must live in exile until Israel is perfectly Torah observant.

Of course, this conundrum would be made even greater if every Torah observant Jew felt this way. This would mean that all Torah observant Jews must steer clear of Israel until all the secular Jews — the only ones who would populate the land — become Torah observant entirely on their own. Once this happens, the more advanced Torah observant Jews would be invited to come and take over.

Only a brilliant Jewish mind can come up with this exit plan, but we all know that Jews are smart.

I am waiting for my community to die

This is the exit plan of most rabbis, as well as other community leaders. Every so often the chief rabbi of some country in Europe, or a prominent rabbi in America, will urge Jews to consider moving to Israel. Presumably, after this brave leader has successfully convinced his entire flock to move, and his vital services are no longer required, he will then turn off the lights, close the door, and follow his flock. His sacrifice in volunteering to be the absolute last Jew to leave his community is most admirable. How could he possibly leave any sooner? He is doing great work and the community needs him.

Of course, everyone else hearing the rabbi's message will understand that it does not apply to them for the very same reason. They are also important members of the community, their contributions are vital, and everything would fall apart without them. So the only people who should heed the call to go to Israel are those who contribute nothing to the community and whose presence would be missed by no one.

Maybe, just maybe, the rabbis are really worried less about the future of their community than their own future. After all, in exile they serve as the great spiritual leaders who keep their community going, keeping alive the dream of one day returning triumphantly to Israel. But the day that triumphant return happens is precisely when these services become obsolete, and they may not find a comparable flock to lead in Israel. These rabbis who are seen as indispensable community leaders in exile might be just another guy in Israel.

Hence it is much better to remain in exile as long as possible, which, for these people, will hopefully be forever. After all, leaders are supposed to follow.

I am waiting until Israel solves its problems (you name it)

These problems may include the government, the bureaucracy, the cost of living, the culture, its resemblance or lack thereof to what a Jewish state should look like, and so much more. This exit plan declares that you would love to live in Israel, and you're moving there the very minute Israel changes to accommodate you. *Kol HaKavod!*

The problem is that Moshiach will come before that happens. Normally that is a figure of speech to mean that it's not going to happen anytime soon, but in this case it's literally true. Moshiach will come before Israel solves all its problems, let alone accommodating all your earthly and spiritual desires.

What this boils down to is the following straightforward question:

How much do you value living in Israel irrespective of your anticipated quality of life — however you define that? Ideally the answer should be "more than anything in the world if only I can get by," and historically that has been the case for our greatest role models. If we are not on their level and cannot make the most extreme sacrifices that they were willing to make, we should at least acknowledge that this is the ideal, and we should be willing to make at least some significant sacrifices.

I would go so far as to suggest that this is part of the reason why acclimating to Israel can be very difficult, at least in the beginning. If Israel were the easiest, safest, and most prosperous place to live in the entire world, it would not mean anything for a Jew to pick himself up and move here.

Indeed, today Israel is a far better place to live on a purely physical level than numerous other countries, and for that reason many gentiles wish to convert and move here strictly to improve their quality of life.

Ultimately, we will all wind up living here one way or another. If the only way that can happen is for life in exile to once again become hellish to the point of despair, so that the quality of life calculation becomes a no-brainer, that can surely be arranged, but it would be a tragic disgrace for it to happen that way.

The truth is that we do not choose where to live strictly based on quality of life considerations. It is generally due more to inertia than anything else. Even moving to a different home in the same city is a hassle, an expense, and fraught with uncertainty. We usually don't move unless we have to (we are forced out, a family crisis, medical reasons) or we have an overwhelming incentive to do so (a great job opportunity, marriage). Barring either a negative reason that compels us to move or a positive reason to inspire us to move, most people will simply stay put.

It really has nothing to do with the government; you probably don't like your local government any more than you like the government in Israel, but you're not going to move because of it. You're also not going to move somewhere else where you admire the government just for that, nor would you turn down your dream job opportunity in a different country because you don't like the government there. Unless we're dealing with a tyrannical government that threatens your safety — and we're not — this simply isn't a factor. So this is really just an excuse.

The fact that Israel is not yet a country without any flaws and shortcomings is actually just the way it is supposed to be right now. It means that YOU have a role to play in making it more like it is supposed to be. For example, if you want Israel to be more religious, coming here as a religious person will make Israel more religious. If you want Israel to become safer, more prosperous, and more successful in whatever areas are most important to you, choosing to live here and build your family here is the best way to help make that happen.

Of course, along the way you might be frustrated many times and might even suffer from the "system." The same might happen if you stay wherever you are. Being that Israel is not a tyrannical country (though injustice is certainly rampant), there is plenty of room for good people with dreams of a better future to help create it.

Even if you are not an influential person, just being here makes the country stronger. Every time you buy something, you are helping a fellow Jew make a living in Israel. Your presence here makes everyone else's presence a little more secure, and strengthens the next Jew in exile that he can make it happen, also.

When Moshiach finally does come, you will be able to say with pride that you were here first and helped pave the way. You came to Israel before it was perfect and made it a little better. You didn't move into a finished product that other people created; you helped create it. Those who come only after Moshiach arrives will hang their heads in shame for being spectators instead of active participants in the building of our land, for choosing to live elsewhere until elsewhere was no longer an option at all.

Israel might not be the absolute cheapest/safest/easiest/most convenient place in the world for you to live today. It might not be a "better deal" than where you currently are. I understand that this matters. I'm also willing to bet that when you add it all up, it's a far better deal than you think.

Chances are that, wherever you are, you are struggling to get by, the bank owns your house and your car, the cost of living as a Jew is crushing, and a few rainy days would drown you. Yet somehow you insist that it's great over there, and in Israel you would starve in the street.

Get real.

The exile is winding down whether you realize it or not, and whether you like it or not. Your days there are numbered, and it's not a huge number. It's time to leave on your terms, for entire communities to plan together how to best wind down the business and relocate to your only true home, and for leaders to truly lead their flock back to Israel, even if it is their final act of leadership.

Israel is still a small enough country that even a few thousand newcomers can make a serious demographic and political change. This is your time to come in groups and make a difference. If you sacrifice some luxuries and comforts along the way, it will mean that much more.

It's not too late to come like a *mensch* and be part of the ultimate chapter of Jewish history. Soon it will be. Stop making excuses, internalize that even a hard life in Israel is better than an easy life in exile (which you don't have anyway), and make a real exit plan.

The land, your people, and Moshiach are all waiting.

The Foolish Prisoner

The *Midrash* to *Koheles* (7:15) relates the following parable: A group of bandits was locked up in jail. One of them dug a tunnel, and they all escaped, except for one who stayed behind. When the warden came by, he began beating him with a rod and said, "What terrible *mazal* you have! The tunnel was before you and didn't escape!"

The *nimshal* concerns a sinner who refrains from doing *teshuva* until he dies and the opportunity to "escape" from his wrongdoing is lost.

Our generation does not need a *nimshal*, however, for we are the characters in the parable. For thousands of years, we were imprisoned in exile, seemingly without any hope of escape. We prayed and pined for the opportunity to be free and return home. That opportunity has finally been presented to us — nearly any Jew on earth who wishes to escape the prison of exile can do so.

Many have heeded the divine call and done just that. There have been difficulties to be sure — crawling through a tunnel is not an easy path to freedom — but they have continued moving forward, always facing forward.

But there are some who have grown used to prison. It's all they've ever known. Prison life isn't always pleasant, but it's familiar. They know the ropes, they have grown used to their role and identity, and their most basic needs are provided for. Prison is safe, stable, even comfortable at times. Prison is home.

Freedom is unknown and frightening. Crawling through the tunnel to freedom means learning how to live differently, to deal with different challenges and dangers, and even getting dirty while you crawl. The prisoner who stays behind cannot bring himself to escape, even when there is nothing stopping him but his own free will.

The warden sees this pathetic person who has lost his very essence and is filled with scorn. He too spends much of his life in prison — but as a free person. He knows the difference between prison life and freedom; he understands that losing one's freedom is the greatest catastrophe that can befall a person, and he can only heap scorn on one who voluntarily chooses imprisonment over real life.

The voluntary prisoner thinks he will be rewarded for his "good behavior," but the warden cannot respect someone who actually *prefers* to be there.

Exile from our homeland is the worst punishment that could have been decreed upon us short of total destruction. Life outside of Israel is life in prison, even in the best of times, even if we are not being persecuted and the prison is beautiful. A true Jew understands that he does not belong there and he does not want to be there any longer than necessary. If he can burrow his way home, he won't think twice.

Millions of Jews have returned home. God made an oath to bring us home, and He is fulfilling it before our eyes. You don't need to be a prophet or a sage to recognize the incredible miracles and clear expression of divine will rapidly unfolding in our time. Those who have been anticipating this moment are embracing the opportunity, even if the journey home is bumpy at times.

Tragically, half of our people are willfully blind to what is happening, though they cover their blindness with rationalizations. Prison life has become comfortable for them, or tolerable, or the tunnel looks too daunting, or inertia is simply too powerful. Perhaps it is the *sitra achara* that is seducing them to reject the opportunity, knowing that when the Jews return home the game is over and we win.

Those who do not return home from inspiration will return from desperation. Those who prefer to stay behind even in times of desperation will find that escape tunnels don't remain open forever.

The warden is coming.

The Galus *Money Trap*

One of the most common reasons/excuses Jews choose to remain in *galus* is monetary considerations. Many are unwilling to compromise on the material standard of living they have become accustomed to. They obsessively compare Israel to *galus* in every materialistic sense, inevitably find it inferior in some area, and triumphantly declare that Israel isn't for them. It is a sad commentary on the spiritual assimilation of many Orthodox Jews.

Others believe that living in Israel all but assures financial ruin. They know someone who made *aliya*, couldn't make a living, and was forced to return to *galus*. Surely if they made the same reckless move, they would join the millions of destitute Jews in Israel who are starving in the streets. They just can't make it in Israel, and there's no point in trying. Echoing the spies who had this notion long before them, "It is a land that consumes its inhabitants."

As Chazal teach us, a falsehood that persists must have an element of truth to it, and this is no exception. Unless someone has a rare level of faith and commitment, it would be irresponsible to make *aliya* without exploring *parnassa* opportunities in advance. Our idealistic actions must be properly grounded in reality.

The problem is when "pragmatism" becomes such a dominant force that idealism is rendered hypothetical.

Torah observant Jews must confront the following questions:

1) What is the monetary value of finally leaving *galus* and returning to our homeland? What price should we be willing to pay, if the privilege of fulfilling this dream was a commodity we needed to purchase?

2) What amount of material upgrade is worth leaving Eretz

Yisrael to dwell in a foreign land?

We are not talking about the extreme case of someone who literally cannot survive in Israel, but those who can live more comfortably outside the land. How much money should be enough to justifiably entice a Jew to leave Israel?

3) In theory, if every Jew could live much more comfortably in *galus*, or received an overwhelming offer to leave the land, could we allow our collective stake in Eretz Yisrael to essentially be bought out? If not, why not? If there is a critical mass that must refuse such a financial enticement, how many people is that, and how are we to decide who must remain as a token Jewish presence?

4) Shouldn't the many impoverished Jews in *galus* — including those with expensive lifestyles who still cannot make ends meet — make *aliya*? Shouldn't the many Jews who use monetary considerations as a reason/excuse to remain in *galus* commit to *aliya* if they were offered a lucrative job in Israel? At what point can we fairly say there isn't anything to lose by trying, or that the risk is minimal enough that idealism should push the needle?

5) How do Torah observant Jews reconcile their "pragmatism" with the fundamental principle that *parnassa* comes from Hashem? On what basis do they believe that their ability to earn a living — and, by direct extension, God's ability to provide the *parnassa* He has decreed for them — depends entirely on their remaining in *galus* indefinitely?

6) Is it not conceivable that the material comforts of *galus* are a test, even a lure of the *yetzer hara* to deter Jews from returning home? How can it be that many Jews consider the miraculous return of millions of Jews to Israel in two generations as "the work of Satan," yet consider the Holocaust the plan of Hashem, and the material comforts of *galus* as a gift from heaven? Is this not a mental illness? Orthodox Jews in *galus* know the Torah perspective to these questions, but they bury it under a grave of rationalizations and deflections. Here it is:

The monetary value of leaving *galus* is inestimable. No amount of material upgrade is worth remaining in *galus*, nor leaving Eretz Yisrael for a more comfortable life. Those who are literally forced out of the land by truly extenuating circumstances should leave with the greatest of anguish and the intense desire to return at the earliest opportunity. This is our law and our tradition.

The notion of allowing ourselves to be bought out of our land for any price is anathema. Throughout history we have bought out interlopers who occupied our land (out of necessity, for lack of ability or courage to expel them). The idea of letting foreigners bribe us to willingly abandon our land is incompatible with Judaism. Every individual Jew who allows material enticements — not absolute necessities — to keep him in exile has sold part of his soul and weakened the entire nation. For what? A bigger home? A fancier car? Cheaper groceries? The Jews in the desert remembered the fish and vegetables they enjoyed as slaves in Egypt, and wished to return. Do we shake our heads at their pettiness, then close the Chumash and emulate it?

As long as a Jew can so much as get by in Israel, he should be unwilling to stay in *galus* for any price. And getting by doesn't mean living a life of excess in the most expensive parts of the country. It means settling the land and finding a way to make it work.

Amazingly enough, and contrary to the common jokes and snide remarks, moving to Israel may even be the best way of preserving one's wealth.

Rav Yissachar Shlomo Teichtal makes an astounding observation in Eim Habanim Semeicha Chapter 3, Section 48. He discusses the Midrashic teaching that Yaacov made himself "like a bridge" to transfer his possessions across the river to save them from falling into the hands of Eisav. Rav Teichtal derives that it is precisely because Yaacov was like a bridge — with only one foot in *galus* and one foot firmly rooted in Israel — that he merited to save his money. All the years that Yaacov was compelled to dwell in *galus*, he had one foot out the door. If not for this — if Yaacov had two feet firmly planted in *galus* — his money would have fallen to Eisav.

Rav Teichtal explains that this is a lesson for the descendants of Yaacov up to our times. Those who turn their thoughts and their hearts away from Israel ultimately lose their money to the *goyim*. Instead of using this money to redeem the land and rebuild it, it goes to Eisav. However, those who have one foot out the door, eager to leave *galus*, have the merit of Eretz Yisrael over their possessions as if they were already there. It is the best financial decision they could ever make!

Remaining in *galus* does not protect a Jew's wealth — it is a primary reason for him to lose it! Rav Teichtal sums it up with the following stinging comment from the sefer Pardes Yosef: "As long as a Jew does not return to his land, and does not sit under his vine and fig tree, his wealth and his business are utterly worthless."

I would add the following teaching from Sanhedrin 112a. The Gemara is discussing an *ir hanidachas*, a city in which the majority of the residents were lured to *avoda zara*. The entire city must be burned to the ground, including the property and possessions of any righteous people who lived in the city.

Rabbi Shimon asks why the Torah said the property of the *tzaddikim* should be destroyed. After all, they did not participate in the *avoda zara*. For all we know, they might have even protested it! Rabbi Shimon answers as follows: "What caused them to live in the midst of the city? Their money. Therefore, their money is lost."

This is a stinging message not just for those who choose to live in a "sin city" for monetary reasons, but for those who choose to remain in *galus* for monetary reasons. Jews who live where they do not belong for the sake of money, at the expense of their spiritual wellbeing and purpose as Jews, acquire a "reverse *segula*" to lose the money anyway.

I am not a prophet, and I cannot guarantee that everyone who moves to Israel will prosper in the immediate future. That is not the way of the world. Nor do I recommend for people to move without making reasonable plans and preparations (though, the way things are going in much of the world, that might soon be advisable). However, the Torah perspective on the money trap of *galus* is clear.

Every Jew in *galus* should have one foot out the door, and strive to lift the other.

The Anti-Semitism Handbook for Diaspora Jews

The continuous rise of anti-Semitic incidents has taken world Jewry by surprise. The nations of the world were supposed to know better and Germany said they're sorry. Yet try as they do to be loved, Jews continue to be hated more than any other population, regardless of what "type" of Jew they are. Wealthy Jews are hated for having too much money, poor Jews are hated for being dirty Jews.

Powerful Jews are hated for controlling the world, weak Jews are hated for being pathetic. Religious Jews are hated for being different, assimilated Jews are hated for being impostors.

Surely this is just a passing phase as it's always been, and Jews shouldn't do anything radical, like returning to their motherland en masse. To help Diaspora Jews respond properly to anti-Semitic incidents of various types, the Jewish Union for Diaspora Eternal (JUDE) has prepared a handbook.

This handbook is the product of extensive research, countless meetings, and millions of dollars in operating expenses. (Please donate generously so our vital work can continue.)

Each section of the handbook lists various levels of anti-Semitic behavior, followed by the appropriate responses. Thanks to our helpful guide, Diaspora Jewry need no longer be confused when faced with the challenges of anti-Semitism, nor overreact and risk making the situation worse. We've had a great run for thousands of years in the Diaspora, and with God's help this will continue. We at JUDE are confident that the best is yet to come.

Stage 1 Anti-Semitism:

- Dirty looks, insults, slurs, assorted other verbal abuse
- Spitting, throwing pennies, assorted other non-physical signs of contempt
- Accusing Israel of racism, war crimes, etc.

Appropriate Responses:

- So what?
- We're in *galus*, it's normal
- It's good to be reminded that we're Jews
- We have to fight hate with love
- They don't really mean it
- It's just kids being kids
- It's fair to criticize Israel
- We have to work harder to educate people and reach out to our neighbors

Stage 2 Anti-Semitism:

- Vandalism of Jewish homes, synagogues, and institutions
- Swastikas
- Desecration of cemeteries
- Jews being knocked down, harassed, lightly assaulted in the street

Appropriate Responses:

- The police will investigate
- Increase patrols and install security cameras
- Probably a prank by kids
- The person was probably drunk or mentally ill
- Create programs in schools about tolerance

- This is an opportunity for the community to come together and show support

Stage 3 Anti-Semitism:

- Holocaust denial
- Holocaust celebration, we will finish what Hitler started
- Bias in the media
- Anti-Semitic cartoons
- Anti-Semitic statements from public officials
- Legal discrimination to keep Jews out (zoning laws, etc.)
- Attempts to ban *shechita*, circumcision, impose anti-Torah curriculum on yeshivas

Appropriate Responses:

- Prove that the Holocaust really did happen
- They don't really mean what they are saying
- Arrange educational events and visits to Holocaust museums
- Write letters, use social media to inform and educate
- Invite the offenders to meet with us and build bridges
- It's not like Germany in 1932, it's completely different
- Use our political influence, work with leaders
- They don't hate us, they just don't understand

Stage 4 Anti-Semitism:

- Attacks on synagogues and Jewish institutions
- Serious beatings
- Children being bullied in school, with no serious consequences
- Fear of being recognizably Jewish

- Occasional shootings and murders
- Expectations of attacks on Jewish holidays, fear of assembling

Appropriate Responses:

- It's a lone wolf
- Try to understand the attackers and their motives
- Increase security
- Train citizens in self-defense
- Train citizens on how to survive shootings
- Urge politicians to speak out
- Express shock, every single time, and insist we won't let it happen again
- It only happens in some areas, isolated incidents, blown out of proportion

Stage 5 Anti-Semitism:

- Pogroms
- Legislation targeting the entire Jewish community
- Confiscation of Jewish property
- Show trials
- Mass incarcerations
- Destruction of synagogues and Jewish institutions

Appropriate Responses:

- It will blow over
- We will use our political influence and connections
- Some Jews have left but we don't recommend it, stay and strengthen the community
- Don't be a fool and abandon your property and your business

- Don't fight, keep a low profile

Stage 6 Anti-Semitism:

- Legislation stripping Jews of basic human rights
- Destruction of entire communities
- Mass murders and other atrocities

Appropriate Responses:

- Hide if you can
- Flee if you can, use whatever you have left to bribe your way out
- Return the moment it all stops and rebuild. This is our home.

The Secret Behind the **Galus** *Jew*

The ability of the Jew to come up with reasons why he will not make *aliya* is truly incredible. It doesn't matter if the Jew is religious or secular, conservative or liberal, rich or poor, Sefardic or Ashkenazic. It doesn't matter what his family situation is, his education, or his background. It doesn't even matter what's going on where he currently lives. If there is one issue that cuts across all divides for the millions of Jews outside their homeland, it is "Anywhere but Israel!"

The sheer breadth of reasons Jews give would lead one to believe that Israel is the absolute worst place on earth to live. They make it sound as if the ever-increasing millions of Jews who do live here and don't wish to leave are crazy (or religious idealists, which to many is the same thing). No one in his right mind would ever want to live in Israel.

At best it's a lifestyle choice, something a Jew should consider "only if it's right for him."

Within the religious world we find intellectual contortions that would be comical if the implications were not tragic. After all, the religious Jew must come to grips with the fact that his daily prayers, his frequent blessings, his religious ceremonies, his holidays, and his holy texts are suffused with love for Israel and the fervent desire to return immediately.

But the religious Jew does not desire this. Not only does he not desire this, he fervently desires the very opposite. His greatest desire is to live anywhere else on earth in a religious cocoon with people who resemble him. His gentile neighbors should think well of Jews, or at least pretend not to mind them, or at the very minimum not persecute them too severely. If things get "too bad" — which is purposely not defined so that the threshold can be repeatedly adjusted as the situation deteriorates — the Jew will dutifully decide that it is time to find another home in the Diaspora.

Nothing inspires a *galus* Jew more than building a new community somewhere in the Diaspora, while nothing turns him off more than the idea of pioneering a new community in Israel. He wants "Moshiach Now" as much as Peace Now wants peace.

So the religious Jew must use all his hair-splitting abilities to do away with volumes of Torah sources that contradict his attachment to *galus*, while taking a handful of convenient sources literally and giving them disproportionate weight. He laughs at Christian missionaries who employ the same tricks to rationalize a conclusion that was pre-determined and cannot be altered.

If you call him on this, he will argue that there are many knowledgeable and pious rabbis who take this position, and he is obediently following them. Oh, the self-sacrifice this poor religious Jew makes to follow his rabbi! How it must eat away at him that he cannot move to Israel because his rabbi said so! Such loyal obedience for rabbis one will not find for any commandment other than the commandment to remain in *galus*.

The religious Jew will not content himself with theological arguments to remain in *galus*. He will supplement his opposition to living in Israel with every materialistic and practical reason you can imagine, and some that you can't. If Israel fails the *gashmiyus* comparison test in any respect, then it would be unreasonable to expect the Jew to move there. Israel must not only be his national homeland and the focal point of his religious practices, but it must pass every *gashmiyus* comparison test. When Israel passes any such test, the *galus* Jew responds, "Yes, but..." and finds another.

There are two simple litmus tests to determine whether a Jew who claims he wants to live in Israel "someday" really means it. The first is how he responds when you counter his reason for not coming.

Do his eyes light up with hope that you are right, that living in Israel really IS more feasible than he might have believed? Does he become excited that his dream of living in Israel might be more realistic than he believed? Does he want to know more, explore your suggestion, and see if that kernel of hope can blossom into a new life in Israel? Or does he immediately fire back with another reason why it can't work?

If he jumps from reason to reason why *aliya* isn't for him, inventing new reasons on the spot if necessary, then clearly he has intermarried with *galus* and does not want to divorce his foreign wife. If he heatedly insists that he just can't make it in Israel, and is upset when someone even suggests otherwise, then he is a *galus* Jew through and through.

The second test is also quite simple. He has given his reason, or litany of reasons, why he cannot make *aliya* today, even though he supposedly wants nothing more. What is he doing to overcome these obstacles?

He claims he cannot find work in Israel. It's impossible to make it in Israel! We will all starve in the streets!

Has he even tried? Was it just a casual conversation in passing, or a serious search? Is he actively and continuously trying to find something? Is he connecting with people in his field, exploring different possibilities? If someone offered him a great job in Israel right now, would he pack up and move? If he lost his job in *galus* and had nothing left to lose, would he try to start over in Israel? If the answer to these questions is no, then he is not giving a reason, but making a convenient excuse.

He claims there are no schools for his children. They will have no future!

Has he even looked? When he visited Israel, did he visit schools? Has he spoken with other parents? If the answer is no, his reason is a farce.

If he is staying in *galus* to take care of an elderly family member, will he commit to *aliya* immediately after his help is no longer needed? If not, he is not staying in *galus* for family reasons, but for something much deeper.

The same is true for every other "reason" that he simply cannot leave *galus*. Actions speak louder than words, and actions that contradict the words nullify the words completely. If they are taking no actions towards furthering their ideal of making *aliya*, and in fact are taking concrete actions to cement their lives in *galus* indefinitely, then they don't really want to live in Israel at all. The excuses they give are nothing more than cover for this blasphemous truth, which many *galus* Jews are still ashamed to admit.

The *galus* Jew will also latch onto the false piety approach. I am waiting for Moshiach! Sure you are. Do you have your suitcase packed like the Chofetz Chaim? Are you saying Tikkun Chatzos every night with tears streaming down your face begging for Moshiach to come so you can leave *galus*? Are you truly heartbroken and crestfallen that Israel is right there waiting for you, but you are supposedly denied entry until Moshiach holds your hand? If so, show it once in a while. You say you are too humble to do that, but you've already blown your cover as one of the 36 hidden *tzaddikim* with the line about waiting for Moshiach. Let's see some emotion — a fraction of the emotion you show when people suggest that you should come now and prepare the land for Moshiach.

The clever *galus* Jew will come up with reasons not to live in Israel that they would be ashamed to apply to any other place. One woman who left Israel, and felt the obligation to defame it as much as possible to justify her decision, claimed that everyone is rude, and she only had negative experiences with the people. Really, millions of Jews of all kinds, but everyone is rude and she only had negative experiences. One can only surmise that if her interactions with literally everyone she encountered were so negative, then perhaps she had something to do with it. I did just that, and she called me a sexist.

You play whatever cards you can.

I can see people moving apartments because the neighbors are rude. I can see people moving to another community that might be more friendly and welcoming. People don't leave countries over this — especially not Jews. Jews have a lot more mental fortitude when it comes to remaining in *galus*, after all, and the *goyim* will have to do much more than be rude to convince them to leave any country in the Diaspora.

Galus Jews are so brave in the face of anti-Semitism — this is our home and we will fight for it! Yet when it comes to living in Israel they are afraid they will get blown up on every bus, stabbed by every Arab, and have rockets rain from the skies more than rains of blessing. Interesting, no?

They cannot live in Israel because the government is corrupt, inept, wasteful, and otherwise unsatisfactory. Yet they would never leave their *galus* land for the same reason, nor is satisfaction with the government a serious consideration when they move from place to place within *galus*. Even Hitler coming to power wasn't enough to motivate Jews to leave Germany, and today's Jews are no wiser. So I'm calling bluff on that one.

They are worried about their safety in Israel. Right. Because the first thing *galus* Jews check when they decide where to live is the crime rate. If safety were their foremost consideration, it's hard to explain why *galus* Jews tend to live in cities with high crime rates, and move in groups to rundown inner cities simply because the real estate is cheap. Safety first!

One *galus* Jew even told me that he believes Jews should stay in *galus* so that if Iran nukes Israel, the Jews in *galus* will survive and keep the Jewish people alive. What self-sacrifice! Staying behind in *galus* just to restart our people when God allows Israel to be nuked! Of course, it makes one wonder why *galus* Jews live in large clusters in places like New York City and communities near the White House, which would be prime targets for large-scale attacks. If the name of the game is spreading out as much as possible to increase our chances of survival, we can do much better than that.

They also claim that there isn't enough land in Israel, or food, or water, were all Jews to come home. The *galus* Jew is staying behind just to make it easier for God, who they seem to believe cannot sustain us all in Israel, even though He did just fine when we were in the desert. Okay, maybe God CAN, but how can we rely on that? We have to do our *hishtadlus* just to be sure. When God sends the Manna from heaven they will return, so we Jews in Israel won't have to worry about food shortages. The religious fervor of these people, their unswerving faith and devotion, is remarkable.

There is only one explanation for the *galus* Jew. He has been overcome by the *yetzer hara*.

Chazal teach that a person does not sin unless a spirit of insanity overcomes him. Indeed, no rational person can learn the Torah, witness the rebirth of Israel, and conclude that God wants him to stay in *galus*. No rational person can see the situation in *galus* declining day after day and resist the idea of leaving as if his life depended on it, when the very opposite is likely true. No rational person will fight for the honor of his foreign stepmother, who at best is only mildly abusive, while he disgraces the birth mother that is yearning for him.

It is the *yetzer hara*. The *yetzer hara* will do anything to get us to commit a sin. He will manipulate us and have our minds play tricks on us to justify wrongdoing. Living in Israel is a transcendent *mitzvah*, and the entire Torah is centered around Israel. Do you think for one moment the *yetzer hara* would not devote every possible effort to convince Jews not to live there? Convincing a Jew to choose *galus* over Israel is the greatest coup for the *yetzer hara*. It is the most logical strategy for the *yetzer hara* to employ, and the only logical explanation for the twisted logic of the *galus* Jew.

I daresay the evil temptation to choose *galus* over Israel is the greatest challenge of our generation. It is irrational, it runs counter to the very essence of the Torah, it requires distorting or ignoring clear divine messages, and it is the greatest impediment to the redemption that is so tantalizingly close. The *yetzer hara* is fighting desperately to keep us with a *galus* mentality, and thereby to prolong the *galus* — a *galus* that has already ended if only we allowed it to be over.

Enough with the excuses. Come home, help us reclaim our land — all of it! — and end the *galus* once and for all.

Courting Israel

Chazal teach that the Land of Israel is acquired with suffering, which is not the best sales pitch for *aliya*. Moving and acclimating to any new environment is difficult, but it seems moving to Israel has a built-in spiritual requirement for the transition to be difficult in the beginning. Why?

Making *aliya* is not like any other relocation. People relocate for many reasons: education, work, marriage, opportunity, health, medical, family, or simply to make a change. Many of these reasons may factor into when one will choose to move to Israel, but it should never be the driving force behind the move. The real reason to move to Israel — and to remain there — is because it is the home of every Jew, and every Jew belongs there.

The process of moving to Israel is, in many ways, like a courtship. There is the infatuation stage, typical of those who come for a trip or a year in seminary and "fall in love" with Israel. In most cases, infatuation quickly wears off, especially because vacationing somewhere and living there are two completely different experiences. The traveler is left with some fond memories and then returns to real life, finding someone else to love.

There are those who develop a greater connection to Israel and wish to visit periodically, for holidays or special occasions. They support the economy as tourists, show support for Israel in various ways, and admire those who "make the leap." Ultimately, however, they are betrothed to another land, and their relationship with Israel can best be described as casual dating.

Then there are those who have a second home in Israel and come for extended visits, maybe even a sabbatical. When push comes to shove, however, their connection with another land is simply too strong to commit to Israel. Their love is strong and sincere, but they are like those who need to see other people, too. They can't be tied down to one person.

Israel is like a beautiful princess with every virtue. Many admire her beauty and praise her virtues, competing for her love. But, like any woman, she wants to be desired not for her beauty and charm, but for her *neshama*. She has to ensure that those who love her are sincere. Her heart is tender, and she does not want to be hurt.

So, like a true princess, she is coy and enigmatic. She does not display all her beauty and bare her soul to all who come to court her — just enough to be tastefully attractive. She tests her suitors to determine whether they are sincere or superficial. She makes them work for her heart, and those who give up easily have proven themselves unworthy of it.

Those who are worthy of her will not be deterred by the challenge of winning her heart. They know that the beauty she allows them to see is only a fraction of her true beauty. They know that the unflattering aspects of her personality are largely a protective shield. She plays hard to get — but she is worth the effort.

Many are discouraged by her defense mechanisms. They call her rude, ugly, immature, unreliable, cold, unlovable. She is none of those things — entirely the opposite — but she will not give herself to those who will abandon her in difficult times. Her suitors must be tested and prove their commitment.

For more than seventy years, the Jewish people have been "dating" Israel. Many have fallen in love with the land and built beautiful lives here — not perfect lives without any problems, for such lives don't exist, but beautiful, deeply satisfying lives.

Many others came not looking for love but with a list of demands, scrutinizing the land with a microscope, sneering at any blemish. This land is not good enough for me, they proclaimed! The land was hurt by their betrayal, and responded with the pride of a true princess. I see many blemishes in you as well, she replied, with no need for a microscope or scrutiny. You are covered in warts from head to toe. I was willing to overlook your faults if you loved me, but since you don't love me, I will make your life intolerable. You can return to your mistress. One day you will realize what you gave up.

Still others have flirted with Israel, enjoyed a dalliance with the land, but can't make a commitment. The land waited patiently for them, offering her love, but has been deeply disappointed by the lack of reciprocity. Like any woman with dignity, she has finally made an ultimatum. You need to decide once and for all. Either settle down with me, or we cannot see each other any further.

For generations the Jewish people have dated Israel. It's time to settle down and get married.

Relating to Israel Under the Erev Rav

Within the world of Torah observant Jews there are two primary schools of thought when it comes to the modern state of Israel — a creation that is decidedly not Torah observant. These two positions could hardly be more divergent from one another. This has resulted in yet another tragic rift within the Orthodox world, which we know is the greatest cause of our suffering from ancient times to the present day.

With God's help we will solve that problem now.

One school of thought is held by those who refer to themselves as "Dati Leumi," or National Religious (I say "refer to themselves" because I have long opposed the use of labels such as these to divide society, poorly categorize people, and encourage herd mentality). This camp views the secular state of Israel as the "first flowering of the redemption," and supports the state with a religious fervor. State institutions and ceremonies are sacrosanct, with the IDF being the holy of holies.

Of course, the fact that this adoring relationship with the secular state is one-sided poses great difficulties for the Dati Leumi. The Erev Rav ruling class has long demonized Jewish pioneers ("settlers") as religious extremists, terrorists, war-mongers, and a danger to the rest of society (almost as bad as people who didn't take the poison shots). The Zionist flowers of redemption have demolished their homes, destroyed their communities, and turned the full force of the state against those who stood in their way. The holy IDF played an indispensable role in these operations, destroying more Jewish communities than all the Arab armies in all the wars since 1948 combined.

In spite of this, the proudest moment in the life of a Dati Leumi is when their son or daughter joins the same IDF. Nothing is more sacred than offering the ultimate "sacrifice" to the state of Israel. If the child was traumatized by having his home demolished (sometimes multiple times), all the better; the sacrifice is compounded.

The Dati Leumi are further vexed by Israel's refusal to allow them to pray at Judaism's holiest site, Har Habayis (the Temple Mount). Israel only permits Jews to ascend Har Habayis in extremely limited numbers at extremely limited hours on extremely limited days. Even then, they are permitted to go up only in small guided groups, which are surrounded by police and Arab Waqf interlopers, who tightly monitor the Jews for any sign of "provocative" behavior. This includes carrying religious articles such as a prayer book, praying out loud, or quietly bowing to God where heaven meets earth.

Any of these activities can be used as a pretext by Arabs to riot and the world to howl, so the appropriate response of the so-called Jewish state is obviously to keep the Jews in their place. Jews who dare act like Jews — or even like normal human beings in a place of worship — are immediately arrested and face the wrath of the state. Teenage girls who wish to pray for sick people had best memorize the names; reading off a paper can be dangerous to their health.

In recent years there has been some improvement. Jewish visitors used to not be allowed to move their lips, lest a prayer escape. Now whispering is allowed, and on a good day you can sneak in a few second-class-citizen prayers in an undertone while the guards look the other way. Like a Marrano or a Refusenik, but in a "Jewish state."

Despite all the above and so much more, the Dati Leumi remain the most ardent supporters of the state and its institutions. After all, they have consecrated this as a religious duty, and religious duties don't have to make sense.

This is why the Dati Leumi observed the covid rules like no other segment of society. They masked themselves and their children as if oxygen were pork, they quarantined again and again, they shut down their synagogues and schools — prayer and Torah study can't hold a candle to serving the state — and they enforced the tyrannical "green passport" with the viciousness of kapos. If the Israeli government declares that touching a Torah can spread disease, then you sooner bury the Torah than touch it, period. And bury the Torah they did.

No matter how much the Dati Leumi are abused and persecuted, they will always continue to serve the state, for that has become their true religion when push comes to shove. What began as noble love for Israel and a desire to be part of the redemption process has morphed into an illogical, self-immolating complex. They complain about their unfair treatment, but continue to support those who mistreat them, for that is their duty.

The Dati Leumi suffer from Stockholm Syndrome. They are unable to recalibrate their understanding of the return to Israel, nor decouple their love of Israel from sheepishly supporting their enemies from within. They look the other way when Israel runs gay parades and promotes perversity, and feel pride when an Israeli wins an Olympic medal, or Eurovision, or a beauty contest, as if this is why God brought us back to the land. Ultimately the Dati Leumi cannot take Israel to the next level; they are just happy to be here.

This is why the Dati Leumi have always been second-class citizens, their rabbis second-rate, and they are scorned by both secular Jews and Charedim. (A secular person who is seeking spirituality or greater Torah observance will not go to a Dati Leumi rabbi.) This is why their children abandon an observant lifestyle in large numbers.

The Dati Leumi camp has run out of steam and has little left to offer.

***

The so-called "Charedi" camp has a polar opposite view of the secular state of Israel, which dates back to the very beginning of the Zionist movement. They understood that the Zionist leaders were hostile to Torah observant Jews and intended to create a state that was antithetical to the Torah. Many of the great rabbis of the time opposed cooperating with the Zionists, despite the deteriorating situation in Europe.

Countless Jews were discouraged from escaping to Israel

when they had the chance, and their blood soaks Europe to this day. Although many "Charedi" Jews subsequently moved to Israel, their relationship with the secular state has continued to be mutually hostile, or indifferent at best. To the Zionists the Charedim are a burden and a threat should their numbers grow, and the Charedim in turn view the Zionists as Hamans with Jewish names. And yet, the promise of government money for Charedi institutions can swing elections and get laws passed.

As the Mafia would say, it's nothing personal, just business.

Aside from this, the Charedim want as little to do with Israeli society as possible. Keeping their children out of the IDF is a life-and-death issue for them. This is largely (but not entirely) because the IDF is a cesspool of spiritual impurity, much of which is deliberately forced upon religious people with the intention of eroding their religious commitment. Even though the IDF offers some accommodations for Charedi soldiers, those who join the IDF are persona non grata in the Charedi world.

Charedim by and large (they cannot all be lumped together, after all) do not see the return of millions of Jews to Israel as a theologically significant event. To them the redemption means one thing and one thing only: Moshiach arrives, brings the rest of the Jews back to Israel, and everyone becomes Charedi.

Charedim certainly recognize the holiness of the land, but, strangely enough, many of them use this as a reason not to live in Israel. After all, they argue, the land is being defiled by all the non-Charedim, and even Charedim cannot handle the awesome responsibility of upholding the holiness of the land. Best to stay away from God's palace, where the penalty for sinning is most severe, and wait for Moshiach to come. Until then, apparently, Israel is only for those who sin the most and those who never sin at all.

While Charedim tend to create stringencies for *mitzvos* — admirable in principle, but often far more than necessary or even appropriate — suddenly they cannot handle the spiritual challenge of living in Israel, and don't even want to try. Better to remain in exile, far from Israel, in places that reek with spiritual impurity, where the challenges of remaining religious are most severe, rather than risk upsetting God by falling short of perfection in Israel. Best to be lenient on the *mitzvah* to live in Israel and all the *mitzvos* that cannot be performed anywhere else. That is the position of many Charedim (or, perhaps, the excuse) who do not consider it God's will for Jews to return home now, even before Moshiach arrives.

Needless to say, the state of Israel reviles the Charedim like no one else. The secular media dutifully blames the Charedim for every ill in society; they have too many children, they are parasites, they contribute nothing to society, they do not respect the rules, they do not care about safety, they spread disease, and on and on.

Canards such as these were historically used to incite pogroms and genocide against the Jewish people. Today in other countries they would be condemned as anti-Semitic. In Israel, however, they are acceptable in polite company, including the government, and a valid reason to persecute huge numbers of people who, for the most part, are righteous, upstanding, contribute greatly to society, and are the cause of no one's problems, despite preferring to keep to themselves.

The Dati Leumi, for their part, side with the anti-Semites on this one. No surprise there! Charedim will sacrifice just about everything for their principles. The Dati Leumi sacrifice their principles for the Zionist state and approval from secular society.

In general Charedim would prefer to live their entire lives without encountering anyone who isn't Charedi. They wish for their neighborhoods to be independent enclaves of "authentic Judaism," where they can study Torah and wait for Moshiach to come.

Since the return to Israel is theologically insignificant to Charedim, the destruction of Gush Katif and other "settlements" doesn't really bother them. They ignore the gay parades because they don't take place in Charedi neighborhoods. They do, however, protest any perceived encroachment on their lifestyle.

The Dati Leumi protest the destruction of settlements, but look the other way at Shabbos desecration and other attacks on the Torah. The Charedim protest the latter, but ignore the former. The Dati Leumi don't protest spiritual atrocities in the IDF, because the IDF is sacrosanct to them. The Charedim don't protest spiritual atrocities in the IDF, because IDF soldiers are irrelevant to them.

What a crazy people we are.

***

The Erev Rav who govern Israel are absolutely thrilled with this dynamic. So long as the Dati Leumi and the Charedim loathe one another, or at least live in completely separate worlds, the Erev Rav are the biggest winners. The religious Jews can squabble among themselves and compete for a slightly larger share of the pie, while ensuring that religious Jewry as a whole never achieves actual power.

The Erev Rav can destroy Gush Katif and other settlements, because the Charedim won't protest, and the Dati Leumi are too weak to stop it. The Erev Rav can destroy Dati Leumi yeshivos, because the Charedim won't consider that an assault on the Torah; Dati Leumi yeshivos aren't real yeshivos to them. The Erev Rav can beat and arrest Jews on Har Habayis, because the Charedim have enshrined the Kotel as Judaism's holiest site and abandoned Har Habayis to the Arabs.

At the same time, the Erev Rav can persecute the Charedim, because the Dati Leumi will whitewash it, and even justify it. The Erev Rav can murder Charedim in Meron, and the Dati Leumi will echo the narrative that the Charedim were at fault, that they are wild animals who trampled one another. The Erev Rav can beat Charedi protestors, and the Dati Leumi will not care; they only care when Dati Leumi protestors are beaten. The Erev Rav can wage war on Charedi yeshivos, and the Dati Leumi will not care; it isn't "their" yeshivos.

What goes around comes around.

***

Both camps have an element of truth, but have become prisoners of their social identities and expectations. Give me a Dati Leumi with the Charedi's unswerving commitment to Torah and his principles. Give me a Charedi with the Dati Leumi's desire to be part of Israeli society today, imperfect as it is. Now we're talking.

It is clear from the Torah that Hashem intended for the Jews to return to Israel in large numbers, and govern the land, before Moshiach comes. The prophecies about Gog Umagog are all predicated on this; they simply don't make sense if the God-fearing Jews are living as subjects in foreign lands. I have written extensively about this, particularly in my book *Go Up Like a Wall*.

Those who reject the return of Israel to the Jews as theologically insignificant because the Erev Rav are in control are terribly mistaken. God wants us to be here and this is not yet the actual redemption. The Erev Rav are not the first flowering of the redemption, but the final obstacle.

However, for this obstacle to be overcome, we need to be here and be in the game.

The Dati Leumi need to recognize that the secular state of Israel, which has been trampling all over them, destroying their homes, forbidding them to pray on Har Habayis, and sending their children off to be killed, while treating their enemies with kid gloves, is not worthy of their support. They can do this without sacrificing one iota of their love for the Land of Israel and the people of Israel, or any of their belief that this return to Israel is the real deal. They need to stop being useful idiots and compliant sheep.

The Charedim need to recognize that this return to Israel is the real deal, and is one of the most theologically significant events in history. They can do this without sacrificing one iota of their commitment to Torah observance or whitewashing the crimes of those who physically rebuilt the land. There are many reasons why Hashem chose them to rebuild the land. If we can accept the Holocaust as Hashem's will, we should be able to accept the rebuilding of Israel as Hashem's will — even if we dislike the agents He chose.

Most of all, the Dati Leumi and the Charedim need to drop the shtick, stop digging in their heels as a reaction to one another, and figure out how to get together. There are many Dati Leumi who have extremely strong commitments to Torah observance and many Charedim who participate in society. They would be almost indistinguishable if not for artificial social barriers.

This brings us to the final point. There is no reason for there to be Dati Leumi or Charedi camps at all. Everyone who is committed to Torah observance and loves the Land of Israel is playing for the same team. Their lifestyles and understanding of every issue do not have to be exactly the same. We need to get together on the things that matter most, stop pretending that every issue is worthy of creating a new faction, and leave the details for Moshiach to figure out.

When we do that, he surely will, and the Erev Rav won't stand a chance.

www.ingramcontent.com/pod-product-compliance
Lightning Source LLC
Chambersburg PA
CBHW052143070526
44585CB00017B/1956